I've travelled the world twice over,
Met the famous: saints and sinners,
Poets and artists, kings and queens,
Old stars and hopeful beginners,
I've been where no-one's been before,
Learned secrets from writers and cooks
All with one library ticket
To the wonderful world of books.

A SOLDIER'S INDIA

A record of the author's experiences as a Victorian soldier in India during the 1880s where he went to defend the "jewel in the crown". The central story is a unique account of a 524 mile reconnaissance expedition from Neemuch to Ahmednagar undertaken by the author and four other soldiers of the 26th Field Battery of the Royal Artillery. After many unsuspected adventures in Central India's mountains they staggered into Ahmednagar exhausted, wounded, and lucky to be alive.

CLIFFORD KEATES

A SOLDIER'S INDIA

Complete and Unabridged

ULVERSCROFT
Leicester

First published in Great Britain in 1986 by
Caron Publications Ltd.,
Derbyshire

First Large Print Edition
published January 1988
by arrangement with
Caron Publications Ltd., Derbyshire

British Library CIP Data

Keates, Clifford
A soldier's India.—Large print ed.—
Ulverscroft large print series: non-fiction
1. Great Britain. *Army*—History—
19th century   2. India—History,
Military
I. Title
954.03′54′0924   DS442.5

ISBN 0 7089-1745-3

Published by
F. A. Thorpe (Publishing) Ltd.
Anstey, Leicestershire
Set by Rowland Phototypesetting Ltd.
Bury St. Edmunds, Suffolk
Printed and bound in Great Britain by
T. J. Press (Padstow) Ltd., Padstow, Cornwall

To Sarah:
Some leaves from your Dad's family tree.

List of Illustrations

Acknowledgements

MY thanks are due to Mrs. P. Kattenhorn of the India Office Library for her help in searching for suitable pictures and maps, to Brigadier R. J. Lewendon and the staff of the Royal Artillery Institution for their kindness and assistance, and to Mr. H. R. Polden for making superb copies of photographs in the Institution's archives. I am grateful to Mr. Ray Poole, of Leek and Mr. A. Bowler and Mr. J. Hurd of Stoke-on-Trent for their pictures, and to Mr. J. H. Newton for reading my Prologue and suggesting improvements. Andrew Dilger of King Edward VI High School Stafford used his artistic skills to produce the imaginative illustrations of the soldier's tales and the rescue of Nana, and I hope that readers will be as delighted as I was with the results.

What I know of my grandfather I owe entirely to my late Aunts, the Misses Keates and Mrs. M. Asher, and to my mother, Mrs. Betty Fisher, the only one of Clifford's daughters who will see their father's work published at last. My wife Isobel and daughter Sarah deserve my thanks for their patience and interest during the past eighteen months; and Mr. Robert Mulholland and the Staff of Caron Publications have given their most thoughtful attention to the presentation of this book. I am sure that my grandfather would have been well pleased with the quality of the production.

Michael J. Fisher

Introduction

by Michael J. Fisher, MA

GRANDPA KEATES died 25 years before I was born, yet he has been as real to me as any of my living relatives. As a small boy I stood in awe of the uniformed figure staring down at me from its carved oak frame in my aunts' house.

I was told that he had spent seven years in India as a Reconnaissance Clerk with the Royal Artillery, and was shown some of his drawings, paintings and other *memorabilia* including a fearsome-looking *tulwar* or native sword. Many tales were told about him: how, out of sheer devilment, he once took a horse into his in-laws' house and paraded it round the kitchen table; and how he gave the local school-master, Samuel "Bug-whiskers" Scholes, a military-style dressing-down for cutting off a lock of his youngest daughter's hair which had accidentally tangled around the unfortunate man's coat-button.

These, and other aspects of my grandfather's character, come to life in the pages of his collected writings which, as I grew older, I was allowed to peruse. Completed in India in 1891, this 536-page manuscript was treasured by my grandmother after Clifford's death in 1917, and then by four maiden aunts who continued to live in their parents' house until the last of them died in 1983.

Now that the manuscript has been handed down to me, I wish to fulfil what was clearly my grandfather's original intention to publish his reflections on a soldier's life. Thousands of men went out to India in the 1880s and '90s to defend that bright jewel in Victoria's Imperial Crown, but few of them recorded their exploits, thoughts and feelings in such detail. A rare, if not unique collection, Clifford Keates' *Flashes of Light From the Storm of Life* is all the more remarkable in that it came from the pen of one who came out of the Army with neither rank nor medal, and with only a third-class certificate of education!

A Soldier's India represents only a part of Clifford Keates' manuscripts: those parts which relate directly to his years in India. The principal item is an account of a Battery March. This is prefaced by two verses which reveal Clifford's thoughts on leaving England and the girl who was his life's love. The book concludes with verses reflecting the comradeship of soldiers on foreign service, and Clifford's feelings on the news of his father's death.

In editing my grandfather's journal I have made very few alterations. Place-names, for example, are given their nineteenth-century form, and where necessary the modern version is given in brackets. The text is also unexpurgated in the sense that it contains expressions and remarks which, though nowadays they would be considered "racist", were commonplace a century ago. We are, after all, dealing with a period-piece which reflects the thoughts and attitudes of soldiers in the days of the Empire. Clifford Keates was, however, one of the more enlightened ones. He took the trouble to read about India, to try to understand the customs and folk-lore of the people he lived amongst for seven years, and even to learn some Hindustani; and according to my late Aunts, he returned to England convinced that there would be no lasting peace in India until the British left it for good.

Though winds may chide,
And seas devide,
Still i'll be true to thee love.

Prologue

CLIFFORD KEATES was born at Leek, Staffordshire, on September 17th 1864, the eldest child of Thomas and Myra Keates. Myra (née Johnson), came originally from Uttoxeter High Wood. They had nine more children, three of whom died in infancy. Their second son, George, followed his brother Clifford into the Army, but he was accidentally killed while on sentry duty at the Canadian Docks, Liverpool.

Little is known of Clifford's childhood, spent in the days before even elementary education was universal, free or compulsory, but we do know that he went to school, that he hated it, and, on his own admission, upset his parents by his careless and ungrateful attitude.

The town of Leek was, by the 1860s, well-served by church schools and a grammar school established by the Earl of Macclesfield in the early 18th century, so we must imagine that it was in one of these institutions that Clifford Keates endured what he later described as "those once distasteful lessons". Distasteful they may have been, but they could not have been entirely wasted, for Clifford's writings reveal an engaging prose and verse style, extensive vocabulary, fine penmanship and precious few spelling mistakes. Painting and drawing were among his other skills, and these, together with keen powers of observation, were to serve him well during his army career.

Whether through want of formal educational qualifications or lack of opportunity, Clifford did not initially find work in which he could use his literary and artistic talents. By the 1880s the Keates family had moved to Leicester, where Clifford was apprenticed as a carpenter and joiner. The family did not, however, lose contact with friends in Leek, among whom were Micah and Hannah Carding, of 3, Market Place, whose eldest daughter, Ellen, was Clifford's childhood sweetheart and future bride.

Several pieces of furniture and decorative woodwork have survived as testimony to Clifford's fine workmanship, but he had an adventurous spirit which the daily routine of plane and chisel could not satisfy. In 1887 a wave of patriotic fervour swept the country as Queen Victoria celebrated her Golden Jubilee, and many a young man was moved to enlist for the Army.

Despite his parents' misgivings, Clifford decided to join the Royal Artillery, and after enlistment at Warwick in September 1887, this 22-year-old volunteer was sent to join the Field Battery, First Brigade RA at Newcastle-on-Tyne. "Light brown hair, fair complexion, blue eyes, tattoo on the right forearm" is the description given in his army record. He stood only 5ft 4½ ins tall and weighed just over 9 stone, yet he was no weakling, as his career in India was to show.

On joining the Battery he was designated as a driver, which in the days before motor vehicles meant working with the horses which pulled the heavy field-guns.

He seems to have had a way with horses, for as a fellow-driver wrote, ". . . there isn't any other man in the Battery what would ride his horses, they are so wild and vicious, but he would ride on a tiger if you would let him". There was indeed a "daredevil" side to Clifford's character, but also a good deal of genuine bravery and courage, as is illustrated by his crossing of the mile-wide River Nerbudda (p. 69) and his heroic rescue of a native girl from the jaws of a crocodile (p. 91).

Ellen Carding remained in far-away Leek and he sent her verses and hand-painted cards. They were determined not to lose sight of each other and their long-distance courtship is one of the extraordinary features of Clifford's story.

In August 1888 news came that the First Brigade was to prepare for embarkation to Central India. This meant that whatever plans Clifford and Ellen may have had in mind for their future happiness had to be deferred, and there was more than an outside chance that they might never see each other again.

From August 22nd until September 19th Clifford was absent without leave, rejoining the Battery at Newcastle a few days prior to embarkation on board HM

Troopship *Malabar*. There is no record of what disciplinary action, if any, was consequently taken, but it requires little imagination to conjecture where Clifford went, and why, during those four weeks.

After visiting the family home in Leicester and saying what was to be his last farewell to his father, he would have gone to Leek to see Ellen and her family, and this may have been the occasion when he presented her with the gold engagement ring, set with tiny pearls, which is now a family heirloom. That Ellen should accompany Clifford to India was out of the question, and although the Cardings, who owned a plumbing and decorating business in Leek, offered to buy him out of the Army, Clifford refused.

It was not the honourable way out of a career which he had freely chosen and, as his father had said to him, "You have made your bed, now you must lie on it". So, in the young soldier's own words,

". . . a maid with perfect form and
    face,
With heart and mind to match her
    grace.

In tears her lover marched away,
But they shall meet again Some Day".

Meet again they did, but not for another seven years, during which time they kept up a weekly correspondence, Clifford telling his fianceé of the Battery's exploits, and Ellen enclosing copies of the local newspaper, the *Leek Post and Times*.

After a four-week voyage on the *Malabar*, during which Clifford wrote a poem, *Farewell to England*, the Battery landed at Bombay, and from there they travelled to Neemuch (Nimach), some 500 miles to the north-east.

A few weeks earlier, a 19-year-old Hindu from Porbandar had sailed in the opposite direction to begin studying Law at London's Inner Temple. His name was Mohandas Gandhi. Gandhi's career as liberator, statesman and *mahatma* (great soul) of the Indian people lay thirty or more years into the future when Clifford Keates and his fellow Artillerymen arrived at Neemuch in November 1888.

Following the Mutiny of 1857, the government of India had been transferred from the intermediary East India Company directly to the Crown, and in 1877 Queen Victoria had been proclaimed Empress of India, with a Viceroy resident in Calcutta. Some parts of the Empire, including Rajputana (the region in which Neemuch was situated), remained under the indirect rule of over 500 native princes, most of whom had remained loyal to the British during the Mutiny.

The Rajah of Rutlam, who entertained Clifford Keates and his companions in November 1890, was one of several who had been educated in the West. It was hoped that these princes would stand by the British against any future uprisings, for although the period 1858–1890 was one of comparative peace in India, it was an uneasy peace, broken towards the end by violent outbursts of nationalism.

British rule required a strong military presence; even so, places like the city of Mundesore (Mandsaur), mentioned in *Flashes of Light* as the scene of some of the worst atrocities of the Mutiny, were still inaccessible to Europeans, while incidents such as the one described on page 111 are indicative of the tensions existing in many other parts of the country. In 1890 two whole regiments, the Middlesex and the 18th Hussars, and three Artillery Batteries, were stationed at Mhow alone, on the edge of the largest region composed of princely states.

Neemuch lies some 160 miles north of Mhow, beyond the Vindhya mountains and in the heart of a tiger-shooting area. The first Brigade Field Battery remained here until November 1890, by which time it had been re-named the 26th. Field Battery. Though by nature something of a loner, Clifford Keates had made at least one close friend, Jack Mee, whom he had first met in the barrack-room at Newcastle.

Jack came from Ruddington, a large village on the southern outskirts of Nottingham, where he had worked as a groom, an occupation which no doubt helped to determine his Artillery career as a driver. His mother was a widow, and Jack's experience of bereavement was to help Clifford to come to terms with his father's death in August 1889, and with the sorrow and remorse expressed in *A Soldier's Prayer* which Clifford wrote after going into the jungle to hide his grief.

In return, Clifford taught his friend to

read and write, so that Jack was able to send letters home to his mother. One of Jack's attempts at letter writing has survived: a letter he sent to Ellen Carding in the summer of 1889 when, owing to an injury, Clifford was unable to write to her himself.

Although the handwriting does fair justice to Jack's friend and teacher, the spelling is entertainingly odd; but far more important is the impression the letter gives of Clifford Keates as seen through the eyes of his friend:

"Dear Miss i am ast by my chum Mr. Keates to rite you a fue lines as he is in horstital with a bad sholder he was bit by his horse 2 weaks tomorrer . . .

. . . i mite say miss if it aint out of plase that my chum is a gentelman and one that any yung lady mite be proud on for i never saw a man with such nerve he is a faverit with all officers and never mixes up with anybody only me and i dont no wye he shud chuse me for i arnt no skoller but he ses it is my onesty and strate forrard manners . . .

. . . i have been with him in plases

were i wood never go with eny uther man for i allers seem safe with him althou he is very darin he is very corshus and is the envy of all the comrads in his batery for he can do enything and I have herd him say things to officers that uther men wood get 6 months for but they only larf at him . . ."

Both Jack and Clifford were members of an expedition which went out into the jungle for several days in the winter of 1888–9 on what appears to have been a "survival" exercise. Clifford wrote a full account of this expedition and sent it home, followed, a little later, by the skin of a cheetah which almost cost him his life.

The account describes how Clifford while hunting for food found himself looking into the flashing eyes of the cheetah. He fired at its heart and it sprang upon him, hitting him in the chest. They fell from a tree together and, luckily for Clifford, the beast broke its neck in the fall.

He also found time to write a letter to the editor of the *Leek Post and Times*. A Dr. J. Ritchie, the Medical Officer of

Health for Leek, had written to the paper to complain about being disturbed by carol singers during the festive season of 1888. Removed from the comforts of Christmas at home, Clifford wrote back suggesting that the doctor should be transported to some uninhabited island "right away from such petty annoyances—and also from the other Christmas luxuries". Though Ellen Carding may well have been delighted at seeing her fiance's letter in print, one doubts whether Dr. Ritchie was amused by the implication that he was a latter-day Scrooge, or by the suggestion that next Christmas sufferers from nervous irritability should "apply to their model Medical Officer for a strong sleeping draught".

In November and December 1890 the 26th and 17th Field Batteries exchanged stations. In part a training exercise, this involved a march of over 500 miles, with full baggage and equipment, through mountains, desert and jungle, between Neemuch and Ahmednagar.

By this time, Clifford Keates' clerical and artistic talents had come to the attention of his superiors, and he was selected as Clerk to the Reconnaissance Party which was to go ahead of the 26th Field Battery to survey the route and send back daily reports. His work as a Reconnaissance Clerk was to earn him high praise from his Commanding Officer, but he also found time to make his own detailed record of the march, and this is what forms the main item in *Flashes of Light*.

Today this route may be followed by main roads, with bridges across major rivers such as the Nerbudda (Narbada), Tapti and Godovari. How different it was in 1890 becomes clear as one reads Clifford's account of the Reconnaissance Party hacking its way through thick jungle, fording crocodile infested rivers, and languishing across burning sands. Among the many natural obstacles was the great river Nerbudda, whose goddess, it was said, would never suffer it to be bridged—a belief which appeared to have been vindicated by the collapse of the first railway bridge in 1861.

The Reconnaissance Party consisted of five men: one officer, one NCO, the clerk and two messengers. There was also a number of native bearers and guides, the chief of whom, Luximan, acted as cook, interpreter and general factotum. It comes as no surprise to find that Clifford arranged for his friend, Jack Mee, to be included in the party, as one of the messengers. The other messenger was 30-years-old Frederick Lawrey, a Cornishman from St. Austell, who had served in the Merchant Navy before joining the Royal Artillery in 1880. By now an experienced soldier, Lawrey had taken part in the British invasion of Egypt in 1882, and after the decisive battle of Tel-al-Kabir he had received a medal and clasp, and the Khedive's bronze star. After a brief return home, Lawrey had come out to India in 1883, and had joined the Field Battery at Neemuch in March 1888.

The NCO was Corporal James MacDonald another veteran of the Egyptian campaign. In command of the Reconnaissance Party was Lieutenant Frank Oldham.

The Reconnaissance Party left Neemuch on Monday, 3rd. November 1890, followed, a day later, by the Billeting Party. Finally, on the 5th November, the main Battery set out under the command of Major S. Watson, whose wife, the Hon. Mrs. Watson, accompanied him on the march. At Mhow they met the 17th Field Battery on its northward march to Neemuch, and the Reconnaissance Party entered Ahmednagar on December 18th, four days ahead of the main Battery.

On arrival at Ahmednagar, both Clifford Keates and Lt. Oldham were in poor shape owing to exhaustion and wounds received in a skirmish with natives two weeks earlier—an incident which they had attempted to conceal from their superior officers because of the rash conduct which had occasioned it.

As a consequence, their wounds had not received proper treatment, and Clifford almost lost a leg. After a spell in hospital at Kirkee, he returned to active service in Ahmednagar in March 1891, and it was there that he completed *Flashes of Light*, using the notes he had made during the course of the Battery March. Unfortunately few of his paintings and sketches have survived.

From 1892 onwards there was considerable unrest in the north-west provinces as a result of the propaganda activities of the

Hindu patriot Bal Gangadhar Tilak. Rioting broke out in the Bombay area, and troops had to be called out to restore order. The 26th Field Battery was involved in these operations, taking Sirur (43 miles from Poona) from the hands of insurgents. Shortly afterwards, Major H.M. Brackenbury, who had succeeded Major Watson as the Commanding Officer of the 26th Field Battery, received a letter from the General commanding the Bombay Army:

". . . it gives me the greatest pleasure to speak in terms of high satisfaction in mentioning No. 6278 Driver C. Keates of the battery under your command. I cannot but give him the highest praise for his abilities in the field as Reconnaissance Clerk.

His perception is of the keenest, his reconnoitring showing considerable tack, while his observation cannot fail to meet with the ready approval of those connected with this valuable branch of military training.

While attached to my staff this season, I was pleased particularly to note the above-mentioned, and I have found him of exceptional determination and spirit; an indefatigable rider, steady, discreet, and ever ready to convey my dispatches at a moment's notice. And in one instance I was delighted with his speed and discretion in reference to a dispatch which, as you are aware, placed us in that secure position which ultimately placed us in possession of Sirur on the morning of 12/1/93 . . . ."

(Signed) Sir G. Greaves, Bart., KCB, KCMG

From December 1893 until January 1895, Clifford was stationed at Kamptee, some 320 miles north-east of Ahmednagar, and close to the city of Nagpur. From there he was moved to Deolali, near Bombay, a fortnight before leaving for England on board SS *Victoria*: his period of service in India was now at an end. Frederick Lawrey had already gone home, but Jack Mee had another few months to serve in Kamptee before returning to Nottinghamshire in November 1895. All were lucky to have got out of India before the massive outbreak of bubonic plague which struck Bombay in 1896.

One can but imagine the welcome Clifford received on arrival in England, from his widowed mother, brothers and sister Mary in Leicester, and above all from Ellen Carding who had anxiously awaited his return those past seven years.

Now that he had been transferred to 1st Class Army Reserve, wedding plans could be resumed, and Clifford and Ellen were married at St. Edward's Church, Leek, on November 4th 1895 and he resumed his trade as a carpenter and joiner.

Although Clifford continued to do a little painting and drawing, mainly for the amusement of his children, he did no more writing after his return from India. Perhaps he may have looked forward to taking up his pen again after retirement, but he was not so fortunate. The family have always maintained that those seven years in India took more out of him than he would ever admit, but whatever the cause, his health broke down and he died on November 29th 1917 at the age of 53.

Among the family papers there is a black-edged funeral card such as it was once customary to send to relatives and friends. On the envelope, in Ellen Keates' handwriting, are the words, "My Life's Love", which is precisely what he had been, from childhood, through a courtship fraught with anxiety during his seven years' absence on the other side of the world, and in 22 years of marriage.

Ellen died in December 1931, having suffered another sad loss, the death of her only son, Harry, in 1923. Of her six daughters, only two were subsequently married: Mary to a Nottinghamshire chemist, John Asher, and Betty to a near neighbour, Sydney Fisher. Dorothy, Nellie and Flossie took over a wool-shop in Leek, while Myra assumed their mother's role of looking after the house.

Many people in Clifford's home town will remember "The Misses Keates" of 9, Stanley Street, where they remained in business until 1973, and their patience and skill in various branches of needlework. What they will not know until now is that their father was a soldier, author and poet who left behind a rare record of the exploits, thoughts and reflections of a young Artilleryman who "took the

Queen's shilling" in the year of Victoria's Golden Jubilee.

Michael J. Fisher, MA

Some Day

I know not when I'll next meet thee,
I know not will the time be fleet,
I know not when or how 'twill be,
When two fond hearts again will meet;
I only know, deep in my soul,
Your image with life's pulse will stay,
And through dark years that onward
    roll,
My heart will whispering say, "Some
    Day".

I fear my hopes must ruined lie,
Now you no longer linger near.
My heart re-echoes sorrow's sign,
My eye o'erflows the silent tear;
But love! while changing seasons
    move,
While heaven beaming sheds her ray,
This heart will ever constant prove,
And loving hearts must meet—"Some
    Day".

Long, long throughout the weary
  night,
The minstrel bard will sing the lay
Of her, lost to his aching sight,
The loving one he'll meet, "Some
  Day".
"Some Day" when lips, and hands,
  and hearts,
Together meet in fond embrace;
When falt' ring tongue and lip imparts
The love that lived through time and
  space.

Clifford Keates,
On parting from Ellen Carding,
September 1888

Farewell to England

Farewell Mother, Father, Friends,
I must leave you now in tears;
Perhaps for ever, who can say?
But let us hope 'tis but for years.
I know this parting gives you pain,
As o'er life's stormy sea I roam;
My memory e'er shall be with thee,
And her I love so well at home.

Farewell, scenes of byegone days,
Farewell pleasant hours of yore;
I must roam a foreign land,
Guarding India's sunny shore.
But while I am so far away,
No matter what shall go or come,
My memory e'er shall be with thee,
And her I leave behind at home.

Alas! Old England's shores now fade,
Fair Dover's cliffs, alas, farewell!
Though distant now, I still can see

Those clear white tips I love so well.
Ah, who shall say what time may
　　bring?
While I so far away may roam;
But let it bring me weal or woe,
My memory e'er shall be at home.

Now once again I bid farewell
To all I cherish, all I love;
My poor heart yearns for those I leave,
As o'er the bounding waves we move.
No land in sight, the sea so calm,
I think I hear the sweet words come,
Which last I heard when parting from
Those weeping loved ones, now at
　　home.

Clifford Keates

*Composed on board HM Troopship
Malabar, when leaving
England for India, 1888.*

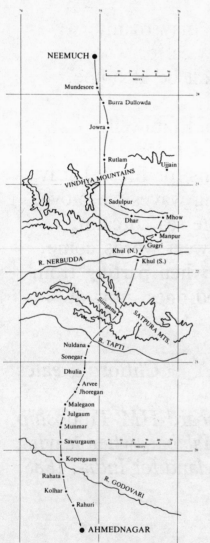

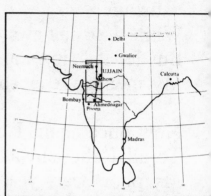

Shaded portion in map (above) shows area in map (left) of the route of the Battery March 524 miles 1 furlong.

The March

Being a full description of a Battery march, accomplished by the 26th. Field Battery, Royal Artillery, between November 5th. and December 21st. 1890 from Neemuch to Ahmednagar, Bombay Presidency, East India.* Distance 524 miles 1 furlong.

DEAR READERS, before I go any farther, it will be as well if I just explain a few little items, which must be properly understood before we commence our "March".

The "Reconnaissance Party", or advance guard, comprises five men, *viz.* 1

---

* The expression "East India" refers to the whole of the Indian Sub. Continent, as distinct from the Caribbean "West Indies" and it recalls the days before 1857 when India was controlled by the East India Company.

1

officer, 1 Non-commissioned officer (Corporal), who interprets between us and the natives, the reconnaissance clerk, and two messengers; we are also accompanied by 1 baggage waggon, and a proper complement of native followers.

The whole of these are two days in advance of the main body (Battery), and one day in advance of the billeting party, and I will here explain briefly the system of keeping the battery well informed, and in the right track. And this being a experimental march, it must be understood there is a great responsibility attached to the Reconnaissance Party, tracking a strange march, as such our duty was.

We take our bearings, jotting down any particular landmark by the way, and by the help of our compass and clinomitor, we ascertain in which direction our destination lies, and drawing a clear map of the true course we pursue, putting down such obstacles as may come in our way. On the reverse of the report, or sketch, we note down particulars of the country, distance of water from camp ground; if fever or any other contagious disease is, or has lately

2

been in the immediate vicinity of the place we wish to make our camp.

Description of camp, and distance of nearest villages, what forage etc. is available for cattle, and sufficient food for native followers. Nearest distance to any railway, or any means of communication with postal districts or military stations.

After the day's march, we send back one messenger with two reports, one for billeting party, and the other for the Battery.

Our rations, comprising tea, sugar and sometimes bread, are brought in by each returning messenger, while our meat is obtained from anyone who has a spare sheep or cow for sale. A sheep costing on average from two to three rupees, sometimes even cheaper, especially if we come across a stray. We have of course to do our own slaughtering. Food for the cattle we have to get from the nearest place possible, as this is of importance for the main body, so long as we procured the regulation quantity for the battery we did not care so much for the beast we rode, as we could gather it ourselves or turn them for an hour into some poor devil's crops.

Having thus far opened the secret of constant communication with the main body, I will now proceed to the more important part of our Duty, "The March", and as you follow me from day to day on this tedious, and never to be forgotten experience, you will see with what troubles and obstacles we were often beset.

Monday 3rd November, 5 a.m.

We saddle our horses and start for the first camp. This is a comparatively easy day's march, being a well-known track, often having traversed it when out jungling. Mr. Oldham and myself in the van, compass and clinomitor before us, our sketch-books and reports handy, to note down any particular item by the way. Though I have often traversed this track before, I never remember enjoying the cool morning breeze so much before; perhaps it was the thought of leaving so unhealthy a station as Neemuch, and on reaching the brow of the hill some two miles further on, we turn and wave a very earnest farewell to so much disliked a place. We descend the opposite slope of the hill and cross the plain beyond to a small stream, where our patient steeds are quite ready to moisten their dusty throats, while their riders are not sorry to wet their whistles from the leathern bottle at their side, which washes down a small sandwich at the same time. Having tightened our girths, we again climb into the saddle and proceed on our way, ascertaining that the baggage waggon is all right, we light our pipes, and settle down for a few miles trot, arriving at Chuldoo by 7-30, thus accomplishing 13 miles 7 furlongs, and our first day's march.

"Now, boys, unharness and picket the horses, then to satisfy the cravings of the inner man", chimes the pleasant voice of Mr. Oldham, "by that time the baggage will be up and the *syces* (grooms) can groom the horses".

By the time the tent is up it begins to get warm, so we bring in the saddles (our pillows), and having spread our blankets beneath the kindly shelter of the tent, we proceed to spend our first day in as pleasant a manner as possible, smoking, drinking tea, and spinning yarns for the chief amusements of the others, while Mr.

Oldham and I make out our daily reports. Dinner having again satisfied the inner man at 2 p.m., we court the sweet influence of sleep, and drown our senses in undisturbed slumbers, till Luximan, our general factotum, informs us that *chah* (tea) is ready.

And now the sun has lost its greater power, we assume our forage caps (field) and stroll in the jungle with our guns to see what luck will do to provide for supper and a bite for the breakfast in the morning. And as it is not too warm, and we do not intend going far, you, my dear readers can don your headgear and accompany us to the silent tower whither we are bound. Now it is my intention, through the march, to confide to you several, or I might say many, peculiarities of this country, each in its proper place; so we will commence by prying into the interior and uses of the silent tower. This is a building, perhaps 30 or 40 feet in diameter, from 20 to 30 feet high, and from 50 to 100 and often 200 feet deep. This solemn place is intended as the repository of dead Parsees (descendents of Persia). They are carried into this round

6

tower through a small, thick, wood and iron door, and laid upon a thick iron grating, they are all but nude, simply having but one white copra or white cloth round their loins; they also keep on all the jewelry which they were used to decking themselves with in life. When time, and the fowls of the air, who by the way descend from the open top of the tower, have completed their work, the bones with their gold and silver adornings drop one by one as they are cleansed of flesh, through the open bars of the grating, and join those of their friends and relatives who have perhaps gone some few hundred years before them, all sharing the one common grave. And it is reported of these places that many contain jewelry to the amount of thousands of rupees.

Now, dear friends, as we have dropped a hare and a few pigeon, and darkness has set in, we will leave you to enjoy your soft and easy bed, while we prepare supper and ease our tired bones on the gentle bosom of Mother Earth, and fancy our pillow is of feathers. Good Night!

Tuesday November 4th.

"Show a leg!" calls the steroneous voice of Corporal McDonald, "Show a leg, boys! Tea is ready." The cry having reached our sleepy ears at last, and having dipped our face and finger-tips in a drop of water, we take our early livener, a drop of tea. We then roll our blankets and great coats which answer as our counterpanes, we saddle our horses, who have just finished their small feed, and start for our second day's march, with a good heart and clear head. Tent struck and baggage started, we turn our backs on Chuldoo and jog merrily on our way, each enjoying the cool morning breeze and a quick smoke.

I am busily engaged taking notes, when Mr. Oldham draws my attention to a drove of fine deer who have just been startled from a corn field where they had been quietly grazing.

"Can you get a shot, Keates? Your carbine is handy, is it not?"

"I think I might intercept them, sir, on the other side of that *jouri* (corn), if I can manage to keep out of their sight. They

8

seem only to have been slightly startled; however, I will try sir!"

So, dismounting and loosing my carbine from its case, I run along the outer edge of the field of high waving jouri, just getting to the bottom corner in time to get a shot, long range, at the three rear animals. Bringing my piece to my shoulder, I fire and am lucky enough to drop a fine young doe, who lies just on the verge of her safety—three yards more and she would have been in the deep *nullah* (ravine) and out of danger.

"I see you dropped her, Keates! She is a beauty; leave Mee to put her on the waggon, with instructions for Luximan to skin and dress her on the road; we'll have a fine roast today if we never have another!"

Mounting our horses, we trot gaily on, talking about everything in general and nothing in particular until we come in sight of Punt Piplia which we intend to make our next camp, if circumstances permit, and on reaching the outskirts, Corporal McDonald ascertains that food and water are good and plentiful, so we . . .

Cease our journey for the day
And look for food and rest.

Punt Piplia is a pretty little place for a
native village, all seems so neat and quiet,
quite a contrast to the generality of Indian
villages, and there seems a sort of superior
style in the little mud huts which form this
unique village. The natives also seem more
respectful, or it is my fancy; however, they
come down with offerings of eggs, milk,
butter, flowers, fruit and many other little
items they knew would tempt our palate;
and it is needless to say that we could not
think of offending them by refusal, so we
did ample justice to their little gifts, for we
were all fairly ravenous after our morning's
ride.

After breakfast we were informed that a
large *tank* (lake) was not far away, so we
took our rods (a large piece of bamboo)
and our lines (a piece of silk cord) of which
we had plenty, and sallied forth to see how
fortune favoured us with the finny tribe,
but we were disappointed to find they did
not care very much for our dainty bait. We
returned to camp with little more than
four pounds of catfish, but this was an

agreeable change for supper, nicely fried in butter and *jouri*.

On reaching camp the luscious odour of something tasty assailed our nostrils, and on inspecting the flesh pots by the fire, we perceived to our great delight that dinner was ready, so we sat down to roast venison and curried stew, with sun cakes and a drop of tea, after which we smoked the dudecu of friendship with the *Boodalis* (old men) of the village, chatting gaily, while listening to the wild though pleasant strains of the Indian bagpipe (*Bujhaudri*). After tea, which was more a byeword today than anything else, Mr. Oldham and I proceeded to make our reports for the morrow's messenger, and as we were to be early astir at dawn on account of a rather long march, we retired to rest as soon as the reflections of Old Sol had faded in the distant horizon.

Wednesday November 5th.

Morning broke calm and peaceful as the generality of Indian dawns do at this time of the year; and after dispatching Jack Mee, one of the messengers, back to the

11

last camp, we struck ours, and entered on our third day's fatigues.

Seven o'clock a.m. found us on the bank of a small river some 50 yards wide, so having watered our horses, we start to cross it. I find that it is not more than from 2½ to 3 feet deep, and fordable with ease. Having crossed and noted particulars on my sketch, we left Corporal McDonald and Lawrey, the other messenger, to see the baggage safely across. We dismounted and started to climb the rugged road of a somewhat steep hill, which proved tedious work, equipped so heavily as we were.

I made note of the horizontal equivalent of this incline, because this is a matter of great importance to a battery as they cannot mount any incline above a certain angle of descent.

After an hour's hard walking we reached the summit and looked down on the plain beyond. Of course, to us, who are constantly used to such sights, it is nothing unusual, and calls for no special comments, but I will just give you the idea of a novice when looking down on a plain as level as a sheet of water, stretching for 8 or 9 miles, without anything to intercept the range of vision. It is a grand sight, and almost fills the heart of even us, with strange ecstasy. What a noble course for a stag hunt; how you could give free scope to a good charger; how our great steeple-chasers at home would glory in such a clean run as is offered to the gaze! But let me hasten to add, for the benefit of would-be witnesses, what a Hell you run through in crossing such a plain. It is all very well, when the sun has not yet shown her face, and the cool morning breeze fanning your rosy cheeks, but across with us in the heat of the day, when the hot winds scorch your very hands and suffo-cate you, both lips and tongue numbed almost beyond feeling, and then pass your opinion upon the lovely stretch of plain, where perhaps for 8 or 9 miles there is not a bush that is large enough to shelter the few grouse which flutter in the air, and often not so much as a thimble-ful of water with which to moisten your parched and burning throat or that of the panting animal you bestride.

You must not believe that all plains are like this one; far from it, for I have crossed many on which you can enjoy the luxurious shade of some spreading banyan or waving palm-grove, or quench your thirst at some ancient and well-shaded well, with water drawn some 200 feet from the bowels of the earth, and so cool and refreshing that one is inclined to echo the sentiments of the poet and say,

"Drink health in wine, thou sons and daughters,

But I'll drink mine in earth's pure waters".

"I say, Keates, do you think it likely there will be water on the other side of that plain? Because it would be advisable to make the camp here and have a longer day tomorrow. We have come a good distance already, and if at the other side we should fail to find water, it will be a terrible march for the Battery".

"Sir, do you see that thin white mist about eight miles to your left front? Here, sir, take my glass. Well, that is the action of the heat on the damp air, and there is no damp sir, where there is not water to make it damp, and if I am not mistaken, it is a large *tank* (lake) too. There must be a village close to it, as they always build their homes close to a *tank*."

"You are right, Keates! I can now see a long streak like a bar of silver; that must be the surface of the water, is it not?"

"Yes! And here comes the baggage, so we will get on." So after shouting the order back to McDonald to trot, we start at a steady pace to cross the plain, reaching the village of Mundesore at 10 a.m., rather tired, thirsty and hungry.

Watering horses, unharnessing, we picket our tired steed, and make a fire, and by the time our baggage came up, the fire was capable of boiling the tea in a very short time; and bringing our ration bag to the fire, we soon had some sun-dried deer-steaks on the embers. Meantime the tent is up, and all's finished for the day, and I assure you none of us felt much inclined for rambling, having travelled 22 miles of very rough country.

After dinner we levelled our glasses on the ancient city of Mundesore—this place is a maiden city, and no European has yet been within the city gates; they are a very dangerous tribe of people, who show very little respect for anyone. It seemed at first as though we should experience no small amount of trouble to get what we required

15

as regards forage, and even on exhibiting our warrants to the Rajah and big men of the place, we failed to elicit any satisfactory answers, or results to our parliance. And if it had not been for the most opportune arrival of the Political Agent of the district, we most certainly should have resorted to sterner measures, for it would have been almost impossible to take our camp any further on that day. However, Captain Lamort, the Political Agent, succeeded in obtaining for us what we failed to procure; and if he had not been in that district, Goodness only knows what would have been the result of our sterner persuasions.

Now just let us look at this city and its surroundings, but I regret to say I cannot take you to the interior, so you will have to be content with what I was able to see of it. Like most large cities in this country, it is enclosed by a tremendous stone wall, some 150 or 160 feet high, with a parapet running round the whole of the inner wall with loopholes to allow the firing of arms upon the enemy. They also possess some large guns, but of very ancient date, though still serviceable. At the back of the city is a beautiful forest, in which every kind of game is to be found, and it was while walking through this forest in the evening that I saw one of the most beautiful sights I could imagine. On the verge of the wood nearest the city is to be seen a beautiful stream, which up to now we had not been cognizant of, and on the banks of this were to be seen hundreds of peafowl strutting up and down with their magnificent tails spread fanwise, and although we were strangers, they did not seem to be at all startled by our presence, clearly proving that they were seldom if ever molested. Mr. Oldham and myself had walked out with our fowling pieces and sketch books to reconnoitre the place, and it was with great difficulty that I was able to take even a quick sketch of the place. I was stopped twice by the natives while sketching the front gates, and was moved on. Of course we got our tempers out but thought it better policy to swallow our wrath, so we said nothing, but I did manage to take a sketch or two while walking.

We had no intention of firing at anything in particular, carrying our pieces

An Indian peacock . . . in this
place as in many others of this
country, the peacock is held as
a Supreme Being . . . On just
perceiving these birds, I
whispered my precautions to
Mr Oldham . . .

more for safety than anything, and though we did not seem to notice anything very particularly, we were still quite aware that some few hundred pairs of glistening eyes were closely watching our every movement; and on closer observation we could see every now and then some dark-skinned native darting flashing glances from under cover of the underbush which was very thick in this place; and wherever we went, we were escorted by some native police, so that you see, had any of us, Corporal McDonald then having joined us, levelled a gun at one of those fowls, there is not the least doubt that we should have been very roughly handled, if no worse, for in this place as in many others of this country, the peafowl is held as a Supreme Being. On first perceiving these birds, I whispered my precautions to Mr. Oldham, for I had heard of the city of Mundesore, which was by the bye, one of the most hostile places in the time of the Mutiny, and here, as in many other places throughout this country can still be seen the little that now remains of the mounds which covered a once brave comrade. When going through my researches for history of the different places of note on the march, I came across the historic notes of Mundesore, but I shall not give a lengthy account of it here, as it will be found in the many books now in print pertaining to the Mutiny. Suffice it to say that on the walls of this city, many of our poor countrymen were cruelly nailed, after suffering some of the most blood-curdling tortures imaginable, and there still remains the tree right opposite the city gates, where over 200 of our countrymen were hanged by the natives. It was here that Wellington astonished the natives by his cool courage, by breaching the outer walls, and slaughtering some four hundred of them with his scathing guns.

On reaching the outer edge of the tope or wood, we were surprised by a large herd of black pig (*suah*), and were entreated by our guides to shoot at them, as they are much averse to these animals as unclean beasts being possessed of the evil spirit; but it was quite impossible to shoot at them for fear of killing some of the natives who on first seeing the pigs instantly fell on their knees and performed some of the most outlandish antics that one would wish to witness, and I am sure, had our sides not been made of tough material, we certainly must have exploded, for I must admit, I have seldom laughed so much in this country, and even now I often smile to myself at the recollection of that day, and the natives seemed as much astonished at our merriment as they were astonished at the appearance of the animals.

We returned to camp, and to supper, after which we sat outside the tent smoking, and anxiously scanning the plain with our night glass, for we expected the return of our first messenger about sunset that evening, and it was now two hours past and quite dark. But we at last gave up all hope of seeing him that night, so we put on the pot for supper, and turned our thoughts to other matters, reports etc.

After supper we decided to walk over to the lake some two or three hundred yards away, and as the moon was up we took our guns in anticipation of a shot at some duck, and as we were straggling along by the edge of the lake, I put my night glasses again to my eyes in hopes I might yet see something of our messenger, when I detected a dark object moving across the plain, but going more to our right. On closer scrutiny I made it out to be a mounted man, so I gave signal (2 shots in quick succession) from a colt, McDonald having brought one with him. This is the signal given when any of the party get astray while reconnoitring. We waited patiently for a few seconds, and were delighted to see two sharp flashes from the object followed by two scarcely audible reports in succession, which told us at once it was our lost messenger returning. I will here give a brief outline of the system in use at present, but could be much improved upon, by which the messenger would be able to trace us two day's march or more ahead, but under the present system they go only by compass or any simply marked object recognisable which we are compelled to leave by the way; thus when darkness overtakes them, they are necessarily compelled to travel slowly, being dismounted to enable them to detect any small mark left by us, very often having nothing but the hoof-prints of our horses, when the ground is of a nature to take an impression, which is invariably the case in this country, except on rocky ground.

Poor old Jack! Pray excuse the expression, but in speaking thus I mean my friend, but let me hasten to explain my reason for doing so. You will doubtless notice often throughout the "Flashes of Light", my allusion to my friend. Though at the commencement of his soldier's career, he had never received the education which would enable him to read or write much beyond his own name, but having chosen him as my companion from the first moment of our meeting in the Barrack Room at Newcastle (on Tyne), I determined then to give him the benefit of my own schooling, which I regret to say has benefited me so little, more, I think from carelessness, and thoughtlessness on my own part in earlier days. But what I did retain of those once distasteful lessons I endeavoured to instil into the ready wits of my chum, and was rewarded by the daily improvement of my pupil, who I now remember once wrote to my friends in England while I was on a severe bed of sickness. I was determined, on learning that I was to take the reconnaissance of the march, to secure my only friend John Mee as the sharer of my joys and troubles in this tedious undertaking, and he, being a willing learner, soon came to understand the duties in which he has proved himself so efficient.

Well, to return to the march. Mee soon reached camp, thirsty, hungry, and completely worn out, as also was the poor beast he rode. However a nice hot supper, with a panakin of good strong tea, put him in a better humour, while his tired steed was cared for as only soldiers' horses are.

"Turn in!" sounded across the still bosom of the lake, as we heard the distant solemn sound of a gong in the village tolling out the hour of nine, so we laid our heads to the pillow, lighted our pipes, and bade the outer world goodnight.

Thursday November 6th.

"Hallo there! Going to lay there while the sun scorches your eyes out? Tea's ready this half hour", came the call from the camp fire, telling us that McDonald was proving his assertion when saying, "I'll be first up in the morn."

Tent struck, baggage packed and started off, we saddled our steeds and followed, and as there is little to notice on this day in particular, we will pitch tent, breakfast, dine, sup and sleep after our usual fashion. I do not intend to notify the dispatch and return of our messengers every day; take it for granted that they are ever on the move. I need not say that today we were quite tired enough, after duty was finished for the day, to avail ourselves of the little rest afforded to us by the hard ground, amusing ourselves with anything which took our fancy most, tobacco of course supplying our chief pleasure, and I do not think it necessary to mention how much of this Balm of Gilead is consumed daily, but we were all smokers, and it being our only solace in weal or woe, we made a couple of pounds look small by the end of the week; but it is very cheap out here, and a good thing too.

Friday November 7th.

Another start is made after dispatching reports, and by the look of the sky, we shall not be surprised if we carry a wet jacket into the next camp. The clouds look purple, and the sun not having yet shown her face, things do not look so bright as we could wish, but our spirits are somewhat raised when, about 6-30, the dark clouds roll away and give place to a brighter atmosphere, the sun having burnt her way through the misty air. We like rain in this country, for everyone knows who has visited East India, we rely on the rain to fill our wells and tanks, and it is indeed a very scarce thing out here except in the Monsoons, which generally last from two to three months. But what we do not care for is a wet skin, especially circumstanced as were were. When in barracks we do not mind a good soaking, but under canvas it is quite different, but I will not damp your spirits with the anticipation of a storm, or my own by referring to those I so well remember on the march.

"What's that, Mr. Oldham? It looks like a bustard, and I believe it is one too. I only saw one or two before in Neemuch."

"You are right, Keates; it is one. It does not see us, does it? Give me your carbine, McDonald, I will see if I can reach her, she's a fine bird. Get on the off side of her, Keates, and take her on the wing if I miss her."

Bang! "Ah, old lady, you have finished pecking", said Oldham as he returned his still smoking carbine to the corporal. "Oh, Luximan, here, pluck and dress this, and have it ready to cook when we reach camp; but isn't she a beauty boys? I never saw a finer bird. Let us have a trot now, boys, and shake a little of this confounded drowsiness out of these horses; they are going to sleep".

"By Jove! That's a fine view over there though: isn't it an idyll (*Ramsami*) or place of worship? That's worth looking at, Keates; it's such an odd-looking place too!"

"No, sir! That's the tomb of some big man, and has been there a deuce of a time too, by the look of it. You see those two jars by the door? Well those speak it to be the resting-place of some departed ruler, and are to hold oil, which burns on all big occasions to keep away evil spirits, and light the departed one through darkness to the better land. Poor ignorant devils! I will just stop and sketch this, sir, it won't take me long. Yonder *toptee tope* (grove) three miles to your right front is where I intend pitching camp today, sir, for I see *dhobies* (water fowl) hovering above, and it looks a nice spot".

"Give me a pipe of tobacco, Keates, before we part. We must get some out today when we unload the baggage. Thanks! Don't be long now!"

Having finished my sketch, I gallop into camp, just as the tent is up, and am by no means sorry to have finished riding. For a couple of days at least I have been inclined to stand than sit, having got the seat of my pants wet when crossing the river the other day, and chafing.

While sitting at breakfast, we were surprised to see a long line of column cranes, circling above our camp, and thinking one would not go down amiss for supper, we hasten to bring our fowling pieces upon them, but it was no use; they were too high. So McDonald had the presence of mind to fetch a carbine and at the second shot succeeded in winging a fine male bird. They are very dangerous things to approach when wounded, as we found out to our cost. Mr. Oldham ran to secure him as soon as he fell, and the bird having dropped on his legs made a desperate lunge with his beak and caught Mr. Oldham by the finger. Though it was no doubt very painful, we could not for the life of us help laughing at his expense, until he straightened our faces with a very savage expletive which I will not put in here. It was quite impossible to release the finger while the bird was living, so I took out my hunting-knife and robbed the vicious creature of its head, and not before I got a severe blow on the eye from its wing. Mr. Oldham had a very nasty finger for a few days, as its beak had crushed the flesh to the bone, severing the skin on both sides. However, these are but trifles, and are soon forgotten. I dressed and bandaged the finger by the aid of the medical chest we brought with us; then we sought to drown the pain in merriment, and succeeded so far as to make him forget the hurt, for a time at least. We managed to crawl through the rest of the day without further mishap. I might add that we got McDonald to bring out his banjo from among the luggage, so that altogether we passed a very enjoyable evening. After supper I made out my reports, closed my books, and thus ended another day.

Saturday November 8th.

Having enjoyed a good night, with the exception of Mr. O., we start for "Fresh fields and pastures new" (sandy ones; quite a ridiculous phrase out here). It happened to be a very long day's march this day; having to pass through three villages before forage could be procured for two days for ourselves and the battery; as you must know we do not march on Sundays. We at last however were lucky enough to get what we required in Jowra, and as we were staying here until Monday we endeavoured to make life a little more pleasant than is possible when moving every day; and I am sure you will not blame us for revelling in what little luxury is obtainable once a week.

We pitched our tent under a tremendous banyan tree, close beside a well of decent water, and reaching from the waggon what little furniture we had with us, viz., two camp stools, a water-keg, and one camp table, we proceeded to make our little frail dwelling look as cheerful as possible, laying some tent bags and old rugs on the floor. We managed to scrape some dry grass together for our beds; we also had a small hurricane lamp suspended from the ridge pole of the tent, and by hanging swords, water bottles, haversacks, canteens and other small items on the roof loops of the tent, we managed to make camp life tolerably pleasant, especially when we got a large bunch of flowers for the table; and we were all well pleased with the effects of our labour.

Now, I implore you, dear readers, not to laugh when I tell you that today is washing-day, and as soon as duty was finished, every man jack went off to the well to wash what few articles had been worn through the week. Young ladies who read these lines perhaps will see some merriment, but I cannot: it is no joke to wash your own clothes with so little convenience; and when we had hanged them out to dry (on the ground) it was not once, twice, or thrice, that we had to race after a refractory shirt, sock or handkerchief which the rude breeze had blown away. After dinner, the clothes being dry, we called a "mothers' meeting" (now I give you permission to laugh), and commenced the intricacies of repairing tents, darning socks, sewing on buttons, etc. etc., and there was more than one of us made a pin-cushion of his fingers; but with all these little anxieties we succeeded in spending a very pleasant afternoon, smoking and chatting as we worked, and we were not behind our compatriots who visit the usual mothers' meetings. We discussed our own little scandals, I assure you.

We dispensed with tea today in order that we might enjoy our supper the better, for our boy had something in the pot which he intended as a surprise for us, and it was a surprise too: curried fish. He had been out fishing and did what we had failed to do a few days back—get a full bag—and we did good justice to his kindness.

Now we are at liberty to enjoy what we call a long sleep in the morning, we decided to pass the evening away with pipes, songs, etc., and to finish up in bed with a good yarn, each man giving us one on the Saturday which should be laid down as his turn; each yarn to be taken from his own life, and not to last less than an hour; and as I thought the tales rather interesting, I shall include them in my story as they occur weekly, and those who read these pages may pass their opinion, but I trust they will not criticise too severely, as we are none of us authors of too interesting novels. I shall try to give them as much in the manner and dialect as they were recited to us, having gained the consent of each member of our party to do so, but I am prohibited to exaggerate.

Of course there was a great deal of haggling as to who should divulge his Life's secret first, and the matter being put to the vote, we waited very patiently for our worthy and much-respected leader Mr. Oldham to commence the series, by giving us one of the best he could call to mind.

Having opened a bottle of "Old Irish" (the first of a dozen), they proceeded to enjoy life in their proper style. I was at this time, and indeed through the march, a total abstainer though I must admit I was often sorely tempted, especially when the water was so scarce and stagnant; often we were reduced to one pint per day, and even less, and this very often scarcely fit for cattle to drink; but I remained firm to my purpose for once.

And now as panakins are filled (mine with hot coffee), and pipes in good going order, I invite you all my dear readers, to come inside and listen to the story which Mr. Oldham told in slashing style, as ever and anon our hearty peals of laughter would vouchsafe; and now as we feel inclined for rest, you will be equally pleased to get to your snug four-poster, so with a hearty "Good-night" we close the first week of our march and the tent door on the sleeping world, and at once lay our heads on the leather pillows with every intention of drowning unpleasant memories in a good night's sleep.

Mr. Oldham's Story

"IT was Merry Xmas time, and I had gone home to spend my holidays. I was 19 years of age at the time, and studying as a cadet in the Military Academy. I was always a mischievous beggar, at least so my sisters said. At the time I speak of there was a certain young lady residing in the village in which we made our home. A merry, generous-hearted girl, too, was Phillis Winsom, and in our younger days she had played me many a trick. My brother James (two years my senior) was at the time rather fond of "Lis" (as she was called,) much to her disgust, poor Jim. Well, on the evening before Christmas Eve, I accidentally overheard part of a little comedy that was to take place on Christmas Eve. This was to the effect that Phillis was to prove the ancient belief in the appearance of supposed sweetheart, etc., etc., and I, feeling inclined for a good joke, did not wish to lose this opportunity of enjoying one.

Christmas Eve at last arrived, with all its ancient cosiness and good fare. I had spent a jolly day helping the girls ("Lis" and my two sisters) to decorate the dear old house with holly, mistletoe etc., and many's the game we had that afternoon. Night at last came, and Lis, who by the way was staying with us for a few days, tripped off to bed with my sisters, and very shortly after we all followed. It was somewhat after eleven o'clock when I heard someone moving about very quietly, and then knew that the girls were setting out for their field of action; so, dressing as quickly as possible, I took from an old linen chest a very large white tablecloth, and having gained the garden lighted my pipe and hastened to the old churchyard, about half a mile distance. I had taken a near cut through a small plantation, so therefore arrived some minutes earlier than the girls. I had just time to throw the cloth over me and stoop behind an old slate tombstone when Lis came humming boldly along the path, and as it was somewhat before twelve midnight, she sat in the old church porch, anxiously awaiting the first stroke of the hour which should reveal to her her future lord and master. At last the old familiar buzz gave warning that the hour of midnight was about to toll the death of another day, and Lis, bare-headed and without her warm shawl, stood ready in racing attitude, and on the first stroke being re-echoed from the old belfry tower, away she rushed round the church repeating the well-known lines:

"Hemp seed, hemp seed I scatter wide,
Show me the one to whom I'll be bride"
And as the eleventh stroke was booming over the distant woods, she turned the corner of the old church, anxiously waiting for the last stroke of the old clock.

Lis was standing with her back to me, and her face to the entrance of the old porch, and as the iron tongue told out the midnight hour, she slowly turned with her face towards the stone behind which I had secreted myself, and as she let her small white apron drop while scattering the last few grains of hemp-seed in my direction, the mystic words for the last time found utterance from her cherry mouth. My heart almost misgave me as I saw the frail figure slowly turn to face me, but then I thought to myself, "She has come for the purpose of seeing something"; so I very steadily commenced to rise from the grave, as it were, behind the old headstone, my arms slowly extending as I did so. She seemed for a moment petrified by the strange apparition, until her tongue found power to give the most piercing shriek I have ever heard, and fell forward, but I stepped from my pedestal just in time to prevent her reaching the ground.

I was not long in seeing she had only fainted, so, tearing off my white covering, I hastily threw it round her seemingly lifeless form, picked her up, and quietly left the graveyard only just in time to escape the eyes of my sisters, whose voices told me they were eagerly scanning the place from the other side of the old stone wall.

Lis was not very heavy, and I being then as strong as a young ox, it did not take me long to bear my burden through the wood and across the fields to her own home. Having laid her on the step of her own home, I gave three very heavy raps with the old iron knocker, and waited only until

I heard someone coming. I dashed from the spot, and reached my own home just in time to discern my sisters hurrying across the field for home. I hurried to my room and having put the table cover away, I hastily undressed and got into bed, just in time to feign sleep when my sisters entered breathless and "woke" me with the news that Phillis Winsom had been spirited away from the churchyard. I told them to go and call Jim but to waken no-one else, while I hurriedly dressed and descended to the kitchen where I waited the coming of the others. We visited the churchyard, but of course we could find no trace of the young lady who so much wished to see her future husband. I could scarcely refrain from laughing at my brother's agitated manner; however, he grasped her hat, shawl, and little basket which lay on the old porch floor, and I thought to myself, if that is being in love, here's one that doesn't intend going in for any of that rubbish!

The following morning was Christmas Day, and after usual good wishes had gone the rounds, my sisters, brother and I walked over to the neat little cottage of widow Winsom to make enquiries about the kidnapped damsel. The neat serving-maid informed us that Miss Phillis was ill this morning. So my sisters went up and ascertained the particulars of the case.

Phillis was indeed ill, and was confined to her bed for many days to come, and on recovery she told us how the spirit came from the grave of one who had dearly loved her, and caught her in his shadowy embrace; and to this day the event, which of course went the round of the village, remains a mystery. Lis firmly believes to this day that it was the spirit of John Urquhart who took her home that early Christmas Morning. I, of course, have no intention of un-deceiving the now Mrs. Phillis Oldham.

That, boys, was the last and jolliest Christmas I spent at home, for I got my appointment just before the following Christmas, so did not go home, and the next one I spent on board HM Troopship Malabar. Good Night, Boys."

Sunday November 9th.

We deserted our virtuous couch at 7 a.m.,

taking a hearty breakfast after the first bath we had enjoyed on the march so far. The morning was quickly passed away in killing and cooking a sheep we had found straying: The poor thing had been tied to the leg of a native, so we released the poor thing, and as we did not want the object on the other end of the cord we did not waken the poor fellow to inform him of our kind action!

We passed the remainder of the day in the manner most becoming a Sabbath, reading from an old newspaper which had been brought by one of the messengers, and in the evening we enjoyed ourselves by singing some of Moody and Sankey's hymns. Supper over, we packed the baggage waggon ready for the morning, and then retired to roost with hopes of a good night's rest.

Monday November 10th.

"Up and dress, boys: time to start!" announced the advent of the commencement of another week's march. Horses saddled and baggage well started, we turn our backs on Jowra, and jog merrily on our way. This was a delightful day's march, so cool and fresh, and our horses stepping out so boldly, that we almost regretted the day's journey coming to an end when we reached Nawlee after a march of 15 miles.

There is scarcely anything of note in this place, or of our doings, so beyond saying that our appetites were good and our hearts light, I shall leave this day to close with a good night's rest and hopes for many more such quiet days.

Tuesday November 11th.

Found us much refreshed on starting for our next camp, and as we were approaching the grand residence of one of the wealthiest men in the Bombay Presidency, we pulled ourselves together, for we wish to look as smart as possible when entering Rutlam (Ratlam), the seat of the Rajah of Rutlam. And we were not surprised on entering the city by the main road, to be met by the Rajah's bodyguard and staff, with an earnest invitation to pay our respects to His Highness, and dine there "à la Blitz" at 4-30 p.m. in the

Palace of Rutlam. It appears that the place was prepared for our coming, having been notified to the effect from Head Quarters, and some miles before we reached the city we could see the scouts eagerly on the watch for our approach, their bright lances glistening in the sun while the scarlet and white pennants waved in the breeze. We were about to pitch our tent and picket our horses, when a neatly-written request in English arrived from the State Secretary of Rutlam, to ask us to make our halt at the Palace, and on my advice Mr. Oldham gave the order to proceed to the palace grounds.

Rutlam is a rather large city, and on going through the place I was surprised to find quite a superior style in the architecture of the place. Our delight knew no bounds when we were shown round the gardens and menagerie. Long groves of oranges and lime trees seemed to stretch for miles, while pineapples, apricots, gwavis, bananas, and indeed almost every kind of fruit was to be seen and tasted. On reaching the menagerie, we were almost afraid to move about, so near were the animals, every kind of which surrounded us. Huge tigers were chained to walls like dogs; two large lions and panthers were chained in a large square room, their bright eyes glistening as they roared our approach. Birds of every kind and colour decked the aviaries with their magnificent plumage, while the hundreds of monkeys kept us in one continual roar of laughter by their many curious antics. Beautiful large marble fountains were to be seen in every nook and corner, and one, which we saw in the dance-room, gained our most earnest attention. On being set in motion, we saw six jets of different kinds of liquid proceeding from a handful of silver arrows held by the fingers of a water-nymph, and the liquid which flowed into gold and marble basins proved, on tasting, to be the best English and foreign wines: while from an ornament in the hair of the figure was diffused the nicest perfume I have ever smelt, falling into a large marble basin in which you can dip your hand or handkerchief at your own sweet will. I can assure you we were very much delighted and also surprised to find so much grandeur in the centre of the broad jungle, and when we were taken through the palace, our astonishment was very hard indeed to hide from the sharp eye of the Rajah's suite.

We did not sit down with the Rajah and family, whose wives were numerous, but were conducted to a suite of apartments sumptuously arranged for the reception of European guests only, and the style in which these rooms were furnished told us plainly that the Rajah's four years' residence in England had been put to a very good purpose. After our return from marking the spot for the camp of the main body, we were invited to an entertainment given by the *Noch Wallahs* of the Palace, and we enjoyed ourselves immensely, what with smoking, drinking and laughing, the Rajah amusing us by relating the experiences of some of the young girls who danced before us. These damsels were well-made and exceedingly graceful, many of them were even beautiful women, who were decked in a long silken shawl some 30 or 40 yards long, and throughout the whole performance this garment was put in different fashions to deck their nude body, sometimes forming a beautiful gossamer-like gown, but partially covering them, prettily twisted round their waists, brought somehow over the right shoulder, across the head, then allowed to fall in graceful folds down the side of their person, forming a beautiful silk wedding-train behind. But the most difficult part of the performance came last, this being as follows:

Twelve golden stands were placed in the centre of the room, on the top of which we saw a glass saucer, and into this was poured some scented oil, then lighted. These formed two distinct circles. After the maidens (which, we were informed, they really were) made their salaams to the Rajah's party, honouring us with the first graceful curtsey, they each one, six in number, placed herself between two lights, and having put something in the flame of her own two lights which gave out a beautiful green light, they commenced to whirl round and round, while they went in and out between the burning lights. Each time they went the round of the circle of lights, a fold of their silk robe was loosened, until they came round for the sixth time, when the whole length of silken fabric was whirling above their head looking like a silken canopy, while the figures themselves were spinning round so rapidly that we could not recognise any likeness to the form of a human being, and we ourselves were so dizzy that we could scarcely stand still on rising. On going round the last time, they all broke into a wild, solemn sort of chant, while the length of silk resumed the shape of an ordinary garment round their shapely forms, alone leaving the breasts, arms, and the lower parts of the legs uncovered. The whole of this feat was accomplished without one of the garments catching fire or one of the stands being over turned. Then to our delight, the pretty damsels handed us scented sweetmeats on a golden salver, and after making their obeisance, retired. The Rajah informed us that these girls were as pure and chaste in their lives now as when they were born, having been brought up from babies in the Rajah's dance school. Some of them have received very good offers of marriage, but they cannot go as they are already married to a profession by bonds that must never be broken on penalty of banishment from among their own people. After drinking the Queen in a drop of good wine, we shook hands with our host who bade us good-bye then, as he would not rise to witness our departure.

The Honourable Mrs. Watson, who, by the bye, accomplished the whole of the march with the battery, cheering the hearts and lives of the men with her pleasant voice, getting up impromptu teetotal sing-songs etc., gave me a detailed account of the grand reception the main body received at the hands of the Rajah. The Temperance choir gave an entertainment at the palace, and enjoyed a good repast the Rajah had provided for them, but I heard afterwards that the Rajah was quite offended by the major's wife refusing the introduction to the Loves of the Rajah's Harem, but Mrs. Watson denies this statement, in so much that the introduction was not even proposed; but be that as it may, the Rajah was heard to confess that the English lady was very contemptuous and proud. But I cannot agree with this opinion.

Wednesday November 12th.

We turn our backs on the hospitable city

of Rutlam, and while we laugh and talk of the many strange things we witnessed, the time gangs merrily on and almost before we are aware of being out of sight of Rutlam, our horses are startled by the shrill whistle of an engine, and as we look up we find ourselves beside the railway station of Beelphauk, on the Grand Indian Peninsular Railway and having marched over eleven miles, we thought we might go farther and fare worse, so decided to pitch our camp at the side of a well of water on the outskirts of this city.

After breakfast, I was very busily employed, for I had reports to dispatch to Mhow, Poona and Neemuch, with full accounts of the march so far, with full details, and it was not till after dark that I had finished, for I had also long reports to leave here for the battery with requests for change of horses, ours needing shoeing. So you will see we had to make up today for our previous day's enjoyment, but we did not grumble.

Thursday November 13th.

Saddling our steeds, we left camp, and I

might say that from the time of leaving Neemuch to reaching Ahmednagar we did not come across a more barren piece of country, for after leaving Beelphauk we scarcely saw a living thing of any description except a few vultures which we frightened from the reeking carcase of a dead camel, and a few stunted bushes not big enough to hide a hare; and on reaching Soojlana after a miserable march of 11 miles, we were not so very prepossessed with the appearance of the site of our camp ground. However, it proved to be more hospitable than would warrant from the outward appearance of the place. We procured some good corn, but where the deuce it grew I cannot say; surely not in such a desert looking place as this, and what on earth the cattle in the district fed upon, it is hard to say unless they do as Mr. Oldham says they do in Egypt; put green spectacles on the cattle and turn them into the desert amongst the bleaching bones and scorching sand!

It is quite impossible to say anything about this place, unless it is to report that at certain unexpected periods, the hot breezes carry death and destruction to this place in the shape of cholera and other fell diseases. And after witnessing the burning of a corpse close by the village, we had no inclination to spend much time in that vicinity, singing the praises and admitting the beauties of a living dead-house.

Friday November 14th.

Once more we gave our mind to the duties of Reconnaissance, and it was here that we met with our first real catastrophe. While crossing a small stream some 2 miles from our next camp, one of the bullocks fell and broke its near fore-leg, and we had to go on to Boralee and procure another one, which proved a tedious undertaking. However, we at last got a young, strong Brahmin bull which answered our purpose very well, and after some little trouble in getting him harnessed to the waggon, we went into camp, just outside Boralee. There is not much interesting matter to relate about this unportentious place; 'tis but a village with a population of 2,000 inhabitants, Houses (*girkoos*) chiefly of mud and straw, so I shall not dwell longer on its merits or failings, and many such place on the march will not receive more notice than the mention of its name, as really some of them scarcely call for such a thing.

Saturday November 15th.

5 a.m. again witnesses our start for another day. After about an hour's good riding we came up with a nice drove of Sambre deer, and being close to them were fortunate enough to get some more venison for dinner, and sufficient for the morrow with a little game which we felt sure would be found at Nagdar where our camp was pitched by the running stream at which we did our week's washing.

Of course we spent Saturday in much the same manner as the previous one, with the exception of enjoying a few hour's jungling in the latter part of the day, adding a few grouse and a couple of brace of partridge to our already well-stocked pantry. And when the evening closed in, and darkness fell, Mr. McDonald gave us the benefit of his musical prowess while we made a return with what vocal ability enabled us to do, in the shape of a few old songs. When bed-time came round, and the "Dear Crater" got under way, pipes filled and all snug in their hard beds, the request was made that someone should divulge another secret, so it fell to the lot of our Guide, whose story we can better imagine than describe.

Sunday November 16th.

Seven o'clock found us up and doing. Breakfast over, we have a look round the place, and bring a few pigeon back with us. We spend a very quiet day for the most part, packing the baggage at 7-30 p.m. We enjoy a quiet smoke after supper, and then turn in.

Monday November 17th.

Camp again struck, we start for our next resting-place, and after a journey through another desert-like district, with much very rough ground, we come to Sadulpur, leaving Nagda 11 miles behind us.

Sadulpur has very little to interest us, and the following day we got to a similar place about 22 miles further on. Opperce has a sort of suburb, Deree, and the two of them would not fill one page, even with minutest details.

Wednesday November 19th.

We had rather a stiff journey, as our tracks lay over vast plains of cultivated ground, which knocks a horse up sooner than anything, and after travelling twelve miles we dropped our weary limbs in the neat little village of Akolia.

This place is a very picturesque one, and indeed, I might say that the beauties of its scenery equal some of the rural districts at home. It lies right in the lap of some very pretty wood-covered hills, and has a beautiful stream running through, and I perceived that the streets and little narrow passages were scrupulously clean, and no obnoxious stench offended our nostrils. It was a perfect pleasure to walk about this place, and I did it the special honour of sketching the village, for the uniformity of its little mud *girkhoos* (houses) struck me as somewhat worthy of note.

I was pretty busy during the whole of

that day, as we were to march into the station of the District Commandant.

Thursday November 20th.

We took up our camp and left the pretty scenery, and when about one mile before entering Mhow, we pulled ourselves together, rubbed down our horses, dusted our appointments and put ourselves in a condition to be criticised by the different troops lying here, and just before entering the station we were met by Colonel Scott, the Commanding Officer, and his Staff. They welcomed us very heartily, giving us great praise for the condition of our cattle and appearances in general, and after complimenting me in the manner in which I had done my work they rode off to see about finding room for us and our horses.

After pegging out the ground for the battery camp, we rode up to the Horse Artillery stables, where good-hearted men waited to take the work of unharnessing and grooming out of our hands, while we were hurried off to the dining hall to have a good feed provided by the RHA. Mr. Oldham, of course, skidaddled to the

Officer's mess, giving me instructions to meet him at the District Office at 10-30 with all my duplicate reports, warrants and receipts.

We all spent a very jolly day, for we had many old friends at Mhow, some of whom had visited us in Neemuch.

I will give a brief description of the District Station of Mhow. It is the headquarters of the district, and contains one regiment of Infantry (Middlesex), one regiment of Cavalry, (18th. Hussars), one RH Battery, one Heavy Battery, and one Elephant Battery, and it was here that we witnessed the grand instincts of the noble animal. They were drilling, as the performance they went through put to shame any of those I ever saw in a circus. One beast, who had committed a crime, was receiving his punishment, forty lashes, which was given him from the steel links of a heavy chain, wielded by a brother elephant. It did seem cruel, but they do drill, and imprisonment, and are lashed, the same as a soldier, their grog (rum) being stopped for the least offence, chaining up to an iron ring for so many days being the punishment for breaking out of the lines. One has every opportunity of judging the wonderful instincts of these animals in Mhow, and you can always make friends by giving them cake, bread or fruit.

We were informed that the Battery was staying here for 3 days when it arrived, as they would change transport and Commissariat with the battery we were relieving from Ahmednagar. So I persuaded Mr. Oldham to remain another day in Mhow to allow our relay of horses from the Battery to reach us before leaving, and he saw the advisability of doing so, as the horses we then rode would have a few day's good rest before taking up their duty in the Battery. So that it was not before—

Saturday November 22nd.

That we started again on our march, with much freshness and new life. And when we arrived at Manpur, the first station in the Mhow Ghats, we were quite eager to enter into the wild life we were sure to experience. So, leaving camp after breakfast, we roamed amongst the wild scenery to our hearts' content. We returned on

Saturday evening with a fine black buck and a few birds, and when supper was over and we had again buried ourselves, we called upon Corporal McDonald from the folds of our blankets to favour us with his most burning secret. So after we had got our pipes going properly, and McDonald had moistened his tongue from a panakin, he cleared his throat, propped up his head with his valise, and commenced his story in the good old-fashioned style, "Well, once upon a time . . ." but nevertheless it has to find a place here, short as it is to listen to.

Mr. McDonald's Story

"WELL, once upon a time, lang afore I came into the army, I was wandering about the north of England, looking for something to do, and one night I was ganging lang a dark lane, when I was stopped by a wee lassie wi' a bairn at the breest, and as we came up by a big hoose, she asked me to tak' the bairn whiles she fetched a wee morsel o' bread. I taks the wee bairn, an' after standin' in the cauld wind for a whiles, I gang t' th' hoose, but nane so muckle could I scan o' its mither, so I had to tak the bairn wi' me, till a hoose awa' up the town shed a glimmer o' light o'er the road. I tapped at the door, and an auld crone came to the door and spiered (asked) me wha' maks it tha naise this hoor o' the neet?

I taks the bairn to the fire, and the cronie picks the wee bit up an' gives it

59

some milk, so I spiered did she ken o' a shop where I cauld get a wee bit o' baccy, an' she taud me doon the road. So I left the bairn wi' her an' never returned.

But as I was gangin' on my way, I met an auld farmer drivin' to the toon, an' I spiers him cauld he find me a wee job the morn's morn. So he said yes. "Now my laddie," says he, "I heerd say that Scots are aye flee foulk, so I gi' thee a trial. Gang doon the lane till ye see a big hoosie o'er a fen, an' I want ye to scan my wifie. I fain would believe mesel' she is the noo bit too bonnie, an' I would catch her wi' a mon I do think maks love to her when I'm awa', so ye gang on an' tell her I sent thee."

I went to the hoose and knocked, and when I told my tale, she gied me a gude drop o' porrige, and after muckle spierin' she showed me my bed in a little room. I was soon in bed, but not asleep, and after listening attentively for an hour, I heard a wee tap at the windy. The door opened, but it was not the voice of the farmer I heard. After the woman had come into my room to see was I asleep, she saw I was and went out again. I cannot tell you all that went on or what was said, but about 10 by the clock another rap came, but to the door this time. On hearing the bustling aboot, I scanned through the key-hole and saw tother mon gettin' in the copper, and just pulled the lid o'er him as the cheery voice of the auld farmer stepped into the room. He came into my room, and seeing I was not sleeping, made me dress and come into the other room and tak' a wee drop o' toddy.

After we talked for some time, the talk got to the topic of evil spirits, an' I spiered him did he ever see the devil raised, an' he said, "Noo, mon". I told him I could raise one if he would fetch me a handful of straw and some dry wood, a good armful. He got me what I wanted, and I put it in the fireplace beneath the copper. I then told the farmer to get a big stick and stand by the copper, and as soon as he saw the devil raise the lid he was to let him have it and show no mercy. You will guess how nervous was the "Gude wifie" all this time. I then struck a match and put it to the straw, and we soon had a good roaring fire. I could scarcely keep from laughing when I heard a restless shuffling and at last it got too warm, and the Devil arose, but sank back unconscious as the farmer's stick fell heavily on his unprotected head. We pulled him out and got him round; when he made some excuse about coming to borrow something. I did not see anything of them again, as I left the next morning after a good breakfast, and received a present of a shilling for my sharpness. And I have good reason to think that the man who visited the farmer's wife got more than he bargained for, and also got a good lesson, which would no doubt give him courage to study a few words in the 10th Commandment. Good Night!"

Sunday November 23rd.

On rising at 6-30 a.m. we were surprised to find ourselves enveloped in a thick mist, which was quite strange feature to witness, but we soon ascertained the cause; the hills surrounding us gave us this clue. After breakfast, composed of curried eggs, grilled pigeon, and suncakes washed down with hot coffee, we went in search of sport, and found it to our cost, for on descending a deep ravine we were about to enter a dark looking cave, when our hearts stood still on hearing a fearful growl which fairly shook the ground we stood on. We turned and fled, scrambling breathlessly up the steep sides of the hill we had descended so leisurely. When we thought we had reached a safe distance we turned to face our enemy, and found to our disgust that it was only a black mountain bear instead of a tiger as we had anticipated, and before he had time to ask our pardon for having so frightened us, he lay in his death agonies with two bullets through him. Mr. Oldham has the skin now, and many's the laugh we have had over that scramble.

Monday November 24th.

We make another start and get further into the high mountains which stretch for miles around us, and my work now becomes very difficult, having constantly to keep my pencil to paper, and for nearly six miles I was compelled to walk while Mr. McDonald led my horse, for I could not hold him up and do my work while descending such steep slopes as now faced us, and we were not sorry to march into Gujri after a tedious march of fourteen miles. And after attending our horses, and pitching the tent, we gave ourselves up to resting exclusively, till tea-time, when we had the first good meal that day. In the evening we went out and sat on the edge of the fearful precipice, about 1,500 feet to the bottom. It was a glorious sight, for we were surrounded by tall, dark-looking mountains, and while Mr. O. and I were making out our reports later on, the howling and roaring of wild animals was something deafening and truly awful, until our *mocadum* (Sergeant of Syces) told us it would be best to keep a big fire burning through the night. So we all turned out and went to the village and got what we could, having to steal most of it as the natives would not give us it, and it being too dangerous to walk about the place and look for it.

It was in this place that poor Jack got upset by some hill banditti, but he stuck his ground well, and gave them a lesson they will not forget. There were four of them, and he used both sword and colts when they dragged him from his horse, he told us when he got into the next camp, where he found us. His face and hands were covered with blood (not his own) and his clothes were torn. He told me privately that he made three of them kiss the dust and join their forefathers, but this is of no consequence as there is a price on their head.

Tuesday November 25th.

We rise again in our usual good spirits, mount our steeds and proceed for our next camp. We push along pretty quickly today, as we expect to cross the river Nerbudda. Nothing of particular note occurs till we reach the banks of the river. We find it very warm on the plains after being in the hills for a few days, and after a ride of 16 miles we came to the Nerbudda; this is the largest river in the Bombay Presidency and at the time of our crossing (in the dry season) was just over one mile broad.

"I think we had better give the horses a drink and feed, sir, have a little refreshment ourselves before entering the water".

"I was just thinking the same thing, Keates! Dismount, water and feed," was then the order which was very quickly obeyed.

"I think the current is very strong in the centre, Keates, don't you? Shall you take a line or go without one?"

"I shall try without one first, sir, but shall take a plumb for sounding the depth".

"I say, Mac, was it above or below the cataracts the native said the *mugga* (crocodile) were lying?"

"Two miles above, and at the bottom of the fall, Keates. Sometimes they wander from the dead water pool above, to the falls, but only when very hungry. One was here a few days ago and took a cow from the bank, but has not been seen since."

"I think I will cross fully equipped, sir, then I shall judge better the advisability of reporting to cross with or without harness."

"Remember, Keates old boy, you are the first private who has ever succeeded in crossing this alone, that is if you reach the other bank in safety."

"Well, sir, you know when duty calls

we must obey, and as my superiors have trusted me with this responsibility of reconnoitring this march, I can but endeavour to do justice to the high honour they have paid me, and sincerely hope to merit their pleasure by successfully accomplishing the difficult task awarded me."

"Good-bye, Keates, and God protect you," were the words of Mr. Oldham as he shook me by the hand, and when the others had performed a like operation I took my horse by the reins and led it to the water's edge.

I doubt, dear readers, if many of you have ever been placed in similar circumstances. I gazed across the cruel waters which were to make or mar my success on the march, and as I watched the rushing torrent whirling past me, my heart swelled with a strange sensation; I must also admit of a stifling sort of feeling in my throat, but not from fear; no, I can thank God and truthfully assert, I never experienced such a thing as fear, except in reference to my Maker; I descend from the wrong stock for that.

You, my readers, if never having experienced such a moment, can perhaps imagine such a thing: thoughts of home, and after offering up a small prayer, and commending my soul to its Maker, I boldly entered the water. My horse, who was rather restless at first soon settled to his work. Our worst struggle was in the centre current. I set his head upstream diagonally to the bank, and when a little more than half way through the current, which was about 150 yards through, we turned our heads downstream diagonally to the bank, and exerting all our strength we soon succeeded in gaining calm water again, both heartily pleased to escape from the boiling, seething torrent behind us; and after 50 minutes hard swimming, both horse and rider gladly mounted the bank in safety, thoroughly fagged. After getting my wind, I took my flag and signalled for the remainder to cross, but to take a more diagonal course; and after I had taken their answer, I took off the harness and my own clothes and laid them in the sun to dry, while I enjoyed a smoke from my pipe which I had taken the precaution to place in my helmet to keep dry.

After putting the baggage, bullocks and

waggon in a boat, two of which are always moored by the bank on the village side, Mr. Oldham, McDonald and Jack Mee entered the water, crossed and gained my side in safety, and after the baggage had been landed, we pitched our tent and laid our things in the sun to dry, while we wrapped our blankets around us and commenced operations for dinner.

It was in the River Nerbudda that poor Frank Viggars was drowned; one of the nicest drivers in the battery. His brother joined the battery the day before we marched from Neemuch. This was the only accident which happened during the crossing of the river. It appears that the poor fellow was very timid, and having loosed the horses' heads while in the current, he was parted from them, and being unable to swim soon sank. I am of the opinion, as also is the Major and several others, that he was taken by a *mugga*, for he went down all at once and was never seen again. I do not blame anyone for it, but there was a little carelessness and inattention of my instruction on the part of the NCO who was in charge of the wheel horses, which were the last to cross. I led the first party over myself, having come back to the river for that purpose. The guns, wagons and baggage crossed in the boats beforementioned, as also did the Commanding officer and Mrs. Watson. It was a hard and very tiring day, I assure you. The battery started at 4-30 a.m., marched to the river (16 miles), had some light refreshment, then crossed the river, reaching the camp ground on the opposite bank, dead tired, thirsty, hungry and dispirited at the sad death of a comrade. It was just dark when the battery marched into the camp, so you can think what a hard day this was. There was only one tent pitched—the Major's. The remainder picketed their horses, took off their harness, merely soaping and oiling it, and after feeding their horses, they wrapped their blankets around them and dropped off to sleep, most of them in their wet clothes, and nearly all without taking any refreshment except a drop of tea or a dram of rum.

I went to the Major's tent, took some light refreshment, and after bidding Mrs. Watson good-bye, I mounted my horse and started for the camp of the Reconnaissance Party at Julwania, a distance of nine-

It was in the River Nerbudda that poor Frank Viggars was drowned . . . taken by a *mugga*, for he went down all at once and was never seen again.

Above: A species of crocodile found only in India—the gavial (*gavialis gangeticus*).

teen miles. Turning my back on Khul (south) and my comrades, I put my horses head to the south and the darkness of night, while I pulled solemnly on my pipe, but it is very little pleasure that I derive from this exercise tonight; my thoughts are none of the pleasantest, and my solitary ride does not tend to lighten my heart of its sadness. One comrade less to greet— how shall I break the news to his chum Lawrey, and Mr. Oldham who is so easily upset? Ah well, those cruel waters roll over one whose earthly troubles are done, but 'tis hard to die so young. I wonder, shall we lose anyone else on the march? Who can say who shall be the next? These, and many other thoughts, along with thoughts of those at home, crowd through my mind on that lonely ride.

I reach Kurampurna about 8-30 p.m., and after giving my horse a drink, I start on the remaining eleven miles which part me from my friends and co-operators.

About 10 o'clock that evening I joined the advance party in camp at Julwania, as you might expect, completely spun up, while my poor jaded horse did not even wait for its harness to be taken off, but dropped down thoroughly exhausted on the grass which my kind companions had spread for weary horse and rider; and after I had fed and watered the beast and taken a little supper, I dropped off to sleep, thinking it better to keep the ill news of

1. Clifford Keates
26th. Field Battery, Royal Artillery, 1887-1895

Flashes of light, from the storm of life,
Lighting the byepaths, long since flown,
Calling in vain for a rest from strife,
Waiting so calmly, for that bright Home.
C.K.

2. Clifford Keates in Royal Artillery Uniform.
Photo taken before Field Battery left for India, 1888.

3. Moving a field gun onto its carriage, c1885.

4. Ellen Carding with her sisters (from left):
Sarah, Ellen, Susan, Myra, Lizzie.

5. Painting of the River Nerbudda, completed by the author in 1895.

6. A group of Parsees (descendants of Persia).

7. Hill people of Central India c1890.

8. A Rajah with members of his Council. Many, like the Rajah of Rutlam, had visited England and adopted Western-style dress.

9. Clifford Keates and Ellen Carding
on their wedding day, November 4, 1895.

the drowning of Viggars to be told in the light of day, when its sadness would be somewhat robbed of its disheartening influence.

I did not mention the fact of our camping at Kurampurna, but it is needless as there is so little of interest in the place; the same with the next camp, so that the last two days' march must find its interest in its own significance.

Friday November 28th.

We rise early as usual, and you may easily believe it was with a severe struggle that I tore myself from my rather soft couch, and even an hour's hard trot failed to clear my limbs of their stiffness, and not before we entered camp at Gir Nuddy did I feel at all like being my old self. However, a good breakfast had the effect of loosening my joints and tongue, so as we sat quietly enjoying our breakfast, I told them the sad tidings of the death of Viggars, which had the effect of making them gloomy for the rest of the day, and strong brave men as we all were, there was above one pair of watery eyes during the day.

The greater part of this day I spent in recopying the particulars of the march over the Nerbudda, the full description of which was to be dispatched to HQ at Poona.

After dinner we re-shod our horses, whose shoes had been somewhat loosened by the long exposure to water, and became useless when doing a couple of days' march after; and as we expected to be in the mountains again the following day, we could not improve upon a rather tedious afternoon's task.

Gir Nuddy is scarcely worth more than a passing notice, as it has only an ancient wall and tower to recommend itself to an artist.

Saturday November 29th.

We again commence the fatigues of another day, but we are glad to find there are no misadventures lurking in this day's march; and after a somewhat pleasanter morning's excercise than has been enjoyed of late, we enter Simgaria, the entrance gates to the Dhulia Ghats, and after going through the usual proceedings occupying the first hour after arrival, we sit down to a nice breakfast of young grouse and curried eggs, plenty of which can be purchased here at 2 annas per dozen. After finishing our report, Mr. O. and I took our guns and went out in quest of sport, leaving McDonald to make our home look decent for tomorrow, as we then intend to make up for the last few days's hardship by spending the greater part of this Day of Rest in our apology for a bed.

After a couple of hours' ramble we returned with a nice young mountain buck and a few birds, which would serve us for the two days, helped out by a couple of ducks Jack had managed to catch while coming from the last camp. Of course we don't steal these things, we only find them straying, and if we happen to find a nice young goat or calf tied up, we of course take pity on the thing and liberate it (Kind-hearted are we not?)!

Our appetites have been completely spoiled by the contents of the camp kettles, we settle down to a bit of washing, which was done by the side of a small lake close to our camp, and while laughing at the various methods of the several ungainly "laundresses" around him, Mr. Oldham lost his balance on the piece of rock he occupied and fell with a loud splash into the water; as you no doubt surmise, causing a general round of merriment from us, in which he himself was forced to join when gaining the bank like a drowned rat.

We close the day in our usual manner, Driver Mee providing the yarn:

Jack's yarn

"WELL, boys, I ain't much of a spouter, and as I never had any sweetheart but my mother (God Bless Her), I can't spin a love story, but perhaps this'll suit you quite as well.

Now, before I came into the Army I was with a gentlemen farmer who did a lot of travelling about one way or another, but more often in a trap, and once when we had been to Melton fair (Melton Mowbray, Leics.) my master had taken more jaw lubrication than was good for him, and the consequence was that when we were a few miles on the return journey home, he fell out at the back of the trap. I pulled up at once and found he was unconscious, so I poured some more brandy down his throat, threw some water on his face from a ditch close by, and in a few minutes was glad to see him coming round. When he was better, we started again, but as he said he could not go much further that night, we should have to stay the night at a certain inn a few miles further on. He informed me this inn did not have a very good character, as a widow kept it who was chiefly patronised by the whole of the poachers and other rough hands of the district, and they say that no traveller ever stops there for the night as it is rumoured that one once lost a lot of money there.

"Now I have a lot of money about me, Jack lad, and don't want to lose it, so this is what we will do. You get out when we come within a few yards of the house, take these few pieces of silver, act the part of a young farmer, and seek a bed at the inn, but do not seem to know me. Then we can watch each other separately and keep our ears open too."

I got out as arranged, and on reaching the inn, found my master comfortably seated by the fire in the little bar parlour, talking to a woman I should never expect to be mixed up in affairs such as those my master spoke of, but alas I have only too often found that appearances are deceitful. The woman and my master both gave me "Good evening" at once, and on my calling for a glass of ale, it was served by the woman with the blandest (whatever that means) smile I ever saw a woman's face disfigured by.

My master had got his bed, so I asked for mine and was told that there was another bed in the same room as my gov'ner, so our luck was in.

While the master was talking to the landlady, I was making faces at a rather nice-looking young girl, whose duty I afterwards learnt was to mix and give customers staying for the night their sleeping-draught. I could see at a glance that she was sort'er gone on me, so I just tumbled to 'er whim and took her on my knee, and we did enjoy ourselves. We had been talking some time when she whispered me to follow her in the yard for a minute, so I did. "Have you got any money about you?" she said. "If so, look well after it tonight. I like you, so I have told you this. That old fool in there doesn't know he's in a den of thieves, but you do, so look out. I am tired of this life. When you have drunk your last glass tonight, pretend to be awful sleepy, and imitate the silly old coon who seems so gone on missus, and if you hear anyone in your room tonight, don't be awake, twig? 'Cos they won't hurt you: they only want the old man's tin. I shall tell 'em you've got none, as I found out by feelin' in your pockets when I found you here asleep. Now lay there, and I will send out one of the lifts, an' he will find you here asleep, d'you twig?"

"Yes," I answered, and at once assumed that delightful position occupied by people when slumbering (those few last words I read in a book!) which means I put it on as I was sleepin'.

The lifts came, and after he had got me on my pins, we went in the house together, and I gave him a "wet" for his kindness.

I can tell you, I watched all around me very closely after this, and when I saw our last glass of grog brought in I called the girl to my side and asked her if this glass contained anything.

"His does, but your'n don't ".

Without her sharp eyes detecting the movement, I changed the position of the glasses and had the satisfaction of knowing that mine had a peculiar taste, so when I got an opportunity I tasted his and found it all right, so I disposed of mine by emptying it in the ash pan, which act was not noticed.

We at last retired, bidding the landlady goodnight, and on reaching our room, knowing that my gov'ner was likely to be asleep very soon, I took the money, which was in a washleather bag, and placed it under the mattress of my bed. After loading a small revolver which my master always carried, I placed it under my pillow; then taking a bag which I had filled with small pebbles beforehand, I put it under his pillow; then I got into my own bed and very patiently waited for the next act on the part of the enemy. I had not long to wait, for about an hour after we had left the bar, which length of time is sufficient for the drug which we were supposed to have taken to do its duty, I was rather startled to notice our bedroom door opening very quietly, until at length it admitted the form of the landlady, and being satisfied as to the genuineness of my slumber, she crossed the room to the other bed, and after ascertaining that the bag was beneath my master's pillow, she very quietly withdrew, leaving me again to darkness and suspense. However, she had not left the room many minutes when my room was illuminated by reflections of a light without the room. I lay there, wondering what was the next item on the programme, when the shadow of two men was thrown on the opposite wall, followed by the men themselves. They cast a passing glance at me, at the same time throwing the glare of a bullseye (lantern) upon my face, and feeling sure that I enjoyed the deep sleep given me by the aid of their doing, they turned to my master's bed, drew out the bag from under his pillow, and gently shook it. You, as easily as I, can judge of their surprise on hearing the dull "jink" of stones instead of the sweet metallic ring of genuine coins.

They laid down the bag, and then commenced rifling his pockets, but to no purpose; nothing valuable could they find, his watch being placed with mine on the narrow windowsill with the money which I had removed from beneath the mattress before getting into bed, thinking that I might possibly drop off to sleep. After about five minutes' fumbling about the bed, they were surprised to see my master waken up, whereupon one of the men raised a big cudgel for the purpose of putting him to sleep again, when I commanded him to desist, at the same time levelling my weapon at them and lighting the candle that stood on a small table by my bedside. They were both so surprised at the turn events had taken that they were deprived of both power of speech and movement, and were soon properly secured by my master and self, and were soon handed over to the police, one of which happened to be passing the house at the time. They both got twelve months' imprisonment at the next Nottingham Assizes, and thus closed one of the most excitable nights I ever spent.

It is needless to say that my master, Mr. Harrison, took an early opportunity of rewarding me for the part I had played in this little drama, and there is not the least doubt that I should now be beneath his hospitable roof, had not fate decreed otherwise. Goodnight!"

"Goodnight, Jack!"

"Goodnight!"

"Goodnight All!"

Sunday November 30th.

"Good morning, Jack. You were not disturbed by burglars last night?"

"No, but those confounded hyenas and jackals kicked up an infernal hubbub, keeping me awake for about an hour; but I say, Keates, what's the *ukom* (order) for today?"

"I don't know, but the boss is awake, so we shall soon know. Good morning Sir!"

"Oh, good morning, boys. What? Up already? Any highwaymen visit you in the night, Mee?"

"No, but that blessed jungle choir did, sir!"

Breakfast was the next thing to think about, which was soon prepared by the skilled hands of Luximan; after which we took a stroll to the *burra ghat*, or big mountain, some six miles to our right, taking our guns with us for the purpose of having a shot should anything turn up in the shape of game.

An hour and a half's sharp walking brought us to our intended lunching place, so, drinking the cold tea, and enjoying the sandwiches we had with us, we started to beat the thick undergrowth about us. Never since I have been in this country did I see so much game in one place: hare after hare scurried across the plain, to the hope of gaining another hiding place before our merciless shot could reach them; and before we had been many minutes among them we had dropped nine or ten very big hares, and thinking we had sufficient, we retraced our steps campwards.

On gaining a small stream we had previously crossed, we were rather startled to see a fine *Eilghi* (wild bull) drinking at the water. As luck would have it, it was ignorant of our approach, so Mr. Oldham levelled his carbine at the animal, fired, and we were glad to see it stumble forward and then fall with a loud splash into the shallow stream. On going up to it, we found it had been shot through the heart and was quite dead.

Now this was indeed a first-rate change in our bill of fare, so we pulled it to the bank, and stripping off our coats, soon had four sharp hunting knives at work to skin and dissect it. After our work was completed, we picked out the most tender parts of its carcase, and each one taking a piece upon his rifle barrel, we proceeded campwards again, entering our tent soon afterwards without further adventure.

The remainder of the day passed very pleasantly. While McDonald gave us a few bars on the fiddle, we exercised our lungs on some of the well-known hymns, bringing back to the minds of all pleasant recollections of the past; and after our early supper, while enjoying the fragrant weed, "Mac" favoured us with some old Scotch ballads, which ended our very pleasant day.

Monday December 1st.

Again we make a start in a new week's adventure and enterprise, and as we are in a very large range of mountains now, we have all our work cut out, as there is unlimited thick jungle for many miles around, and today even, we have very great difficulty in finding a track wide enough to admit of three abreast; and as we continue our march, the underbush and trees become still thicker, and at every few yards we have to mark the trees which will have to be felled by the gunners of the main body, before the battery will be able to proceed.

Hour after hour we push our way through the tangled forest of trees and long creepers, often being for hours in semi-darkness, caused by the thickness of the upper foliage of this dense mass of vegetation.

Now up some steep slope, now down some deep gully where our horses can scarce tread with safety, do we push our entangled way. Large sambre deer, scurrying in one direction, wild boar in another, while every now and then the deep bay of the black wolf told us that our journey was not one of the safest, and for a moment giving a serious thought to our daily messengers' perilous journey as they will have to pass to and from camp with our reports.

After about four hours and a half cutting, struggling and stumbling, we came out on a clear patch in the midst of this deep forest, scarcely more than fifty yards square, and as we are well aware that still much more of this forest is to be traversed, we decide to pitch our camp in this narrow space, though it is scarcely half the size of our usual camp.

After stripping, watering and feeding our tired steeds, we at once proceed to satisfy our own inward cravings from the remains of the wild bull which had been dried and cured for the purpose of impromptu refreshment.

After breakfast which we enjoyed very much at eleven thirty o' clock, we made out our reports, after which Mr. O., who was invariably my companion while reconnoitring, accompanied me on a voyage of discovery. After piercing the wood to the N.E. for some few hundred yards, we became aware that we were not quite alone in this vast jungle, but that it was inhabited by a tribe of people whom we were not previously aware of, indeed thinking that we alone were the sole denizens at present.

It was quite evident from their curious manners that they had been but little if ever in the presence of Europeans, at least the great majority of them, for on our approach, a few women and children who seemingly had been picking wood in the forest, scampered off in wild and ungovernable terror, rending the air with their piercing shrieks; and on our gaining the outskirts of the city of the forest, which I learned was "Dhywad", we were encountered by a hundred or more almost naked human beings, men, women and children.

I made my way up to a white-haired old man who stood some few yards in advance of the others, and on addressing him in Hindoostani, was surprised to find he understood but little of what I said, but on catching a few of the words which he commenced jabbering at me, I at once became aware that the *Marabi Bat* was their language, so in the very few words I had picked up in this language, I succeeded in making him partly understand what I wanted. He, coming to the conclusion that forage was what I enquired after, he led me to the *Girkoo*, or house of the native chief.

I had been for a long time looking at the features of these people, and found out that they were far superior in form and feature to any native I had yet encountered. I even thought them handsome, while the female portion of the tribe were in many instances as well made in proportion as any European I have yet seen in this country, and I truly admired their lithe and graceful movements. They were chiefly exhibiting the greater part of their bodies in a nude state, simply having a very light sort of garment fastened around their waist and extended to a few inches above their knees.

As we approached the village we were "Sallamed" on every side by the wondering natives, and on reaching the village I was quite astounded to see a superior style about the habitations of this tribe. It was evident that it was a quiet, hardworking, and clean tribe, as the neatness of the houses and cleanliness of the streets clearly proved.

After wandering about the village for some time, Mr. O. proposed penetrating the whole of the village, entering the forest beyond; and as we did so we could not but laugh at the elaborate honours shown us, as such we took their conduct to be.

After feasting our eyes on the feminine portion of the concourse surrounding us, we walked sharply to the other extremity of the village. On reaching the outskirts we were again surprised to see a beautiful clear stream, some 80 or 90 yards wide, and on my sounding it, found it to be very deep. But I must here state that never in all my life was I more surprised, than when the point at which we were standing was literally swarming with fish, and when some few women came down to the water's edge we were quite astounded to see the girls actually putting food into the mouths of these fish who I learned were perfectly tame, and to prove the assertion, a girl of some 17 or 18 summers took one from the water, weighing I should think some 4 or 5 pounds, and as she offered it some grains of corn she held in her hand, it opened its mouth and took the proffered food. But as I drew a little closer to the girl who held it, its terror overcame it, and without further ceremony plunged into the water. Now whether it was the sudden act of the fish, or my appearance which startled the girl, I cannot say, but she somehow overbalanced herself and fell headlong into the rushing stream whose current was very rapid I could at once perceive, and if aid was not soon offered she would be hurried down stream. I saw at once that she was terrified at her position, and on hearing the frantic scream of "*Mugga*" (crocodile) from her companions, I had no time to lose, but quickly divesting myself of jack-boots, helmet and coat, I dived into the rushing torrent after running along the bank for some few yards.

Now I could plainly see before entering the water that there was a tremendous current, but was not quite prepared for so severe a struggle as I ultimately experienced. No sooner had I entered the water than I was carried rapidly downstream, beneath overhanging banyan, palm and wild fig trees, and with a few powerful strokes I gained the side of the now almost exhausted girl. Taking a firm hold of her long, luxuriant raven hair, I was just in time to save her from joining the extreme centre of the river, consequently the strongest current. She seemed to know that she was being saved, and frantically endeavoured to catch at me, while I slowly made for the bank, but I could no longer escape her struggles to clasp me, so she threw her arms around me with a strength I would have believed impossible, and clung tightly round me, preventing the freedom to my arms required for regaining the bank. Slowly but surely we were both being carried by the eddy to the centre current: this I could plainly see, and just as I was giving up all hopes of gaining the bank, the loud screams and shouts of Oldham caused me to look across the stream.

Oh God! What a sight for a drowning man. There, not more than twenty yards from us were three dark objects quickly making towards us, which I quickly perceived to be *mugga* or crocodiles. What could I do? Here was I, a drowning man, encumbered by my saturated clothes, and my limbs securely fastened by the clinging girl. The desperation of a drowning being lent me superhuman strength, and by a fearful struggle I released my arms, took the hair of the now insensible girl between my teeth, and struck boldly for the shore. What with the strong current, the weight of my clothes, and my unconscious burden, I was gradually growing more faint. I was some ten or twelve yards from the bank when, Merciful God, what was it I heard snorting and splashing in the water? I was compelled, if the act had cost me my life, to look back, and there, not two yards from me, was a terrible monster with open mouth and distended nostrils, and I could almost fancy I felt his cruel teeth piercing my numbed flesh. Vainly I struggled to gain the shore in time, despising the unmanly thought which for a moment shot through my brain: no, I would not give even a black woman up to the cruel monsters; rather would I die. Then I was all at once nearly blinded by a vivid flash just in front of me, followed by two loud reports in succession; then my hands, feet and whole body became numb; my mouth filled with water, my nostrils vainly striving to expel the sickening liquid which was quickly suffocating me. Tightly I gripped the seemingly dead girl, determined not to lose her, and gradually sank, down, down, down, till I lost consciousness; and then what wild thoughts rushed through my brain for a few moments, then all is a blank.

"No, he's not dead, sir: see, he breathes! I knew I felt the pulsation of his heart, but Gad, he's had a near squeak; but I don't know as I wouldn't have done the same, though I can't swim".

These and other such like phrases

seemed to be spoken by dream-spirits until the loud, "Hallo, old man; near the goal that time; here, drink this!"

I slowly opened my eyes and saw my comrades around me. It was almost dark, but I could partly distinguish objects around me, so at once saw I was in camp lying on my bed with my blankets around me, while outside the tent swarms of the natives stood round eagerly asking after the *Burra Pawnie Rajah* (Great Water Prince), and on gaining my feet in a few minutes after taking a good draught of brandy, I emerged from the tent. Scarcely had I quitted the door than I was beseiged by the wild mob, jabbering, sallaaming, crying, and chanting some unearthly (I suppose it was heavenly) native psalm.

Amidst all this, I learnt that we were invited to a big feast in the village, and before I knew where I was, the natives carried me to a sort of royal seat on a rough, improvised litter, and as soon as I was seated, six stalwart natives raised it on their broad shoulders and headed a gorgeous procession through the village. Never so long as I live shall I forget this strange sight. In the head of the procession were some six or eight young girls carrying blazing torches. Next came from 10 to 12 tum-tums, native guitars, bagpipes and gongs, while three girls walked on either side of my litter with a curiously-fashioned bell in each hand, which never for a moment ceased their ting, ting; while just in rear of my litter walked the girl I had saved, dressed in the purest of white muslin, with a wreath of flowers on her head and a girdle of the same, while her bare legs and arms exhibited some very heavy gold and silver ornaments. After her came the chief, who I learned was her father, also his family, over whose heads were suspended huge feather fans carried by other young girls, as was the case with myself. I cannot say exactly what bird these feathers are from, but if not from ostriches, then from something like them. These, I learnt, were to keep off the myriad night-flies, mosquitoes, etc. All along the road we traversed were stationed other men and women with bright blazing torches, palm leaves, and other trophies of honour, while throughout the darkness came the continual echo of the weird harmony of the native songs.

I have seen many curious and grand sights in different parts of East India, but I never saw anything, either at home or abroad, which equalled this strange sight. The whole surrounding forest was literally glistening with the millions of fireflies darting about, while in the immediate foreground was the weird reflection of the many blazing torches.

At last I was gently lowered to the ground as we arrived in the compound of the chief's *ghirkoo* (house), and on looking about me, I saw that my three friends were being conducted to seats (on the ground) immediately round my own. There was a strange sight, and those who read these pages who have ever travelled in East India will, I know, corroborate my statement in asserting that these sights are without equal for aweful grandness and solemn stateliness, while the simplicity and weirdness of the whole gives it a native perfection unequalled by any English or other European festival.

I sat on the seat, or rather cushion, of honour, this being a sort of round soft cushion covered over by the skin of a large tiger, the head of which rested beneath my feet, while Mr. O. sat on my right, McDonald on my left, while Mee occupied the cushion on the right of Mr. O.

When we were all seated, in a circle made up of some twenty-four big men of the village, the surroundings again re-echoed with the sound of another unearthly chant. Mr. O. said it was infernal, but neither of us know much about it, while some half dozen young women brought in the good things provided for the feast in honour of "*Blighti Rajahs*". This feast was composed, as far as I could guess, of curried eggs, rice, coconut jupattis, beaten fruits, whole fruits, and many varieties of sweetmeat, amongst which the ever-prevalent sugar-cane was liberally dispensed.

The larger mess, or as I suppose they thought, the chief viand, was composed of minced goat's flesh, milk rice, curry, *ghee*, eggs and flour and this was taken from the bowl with our fingers; this to you seems curious no doubt when I tell you that some 24 or 26 hands, black and white, were dipped into the mess, and it was this alone which led me to think these people were of a totally different caste to the numerous other castes throughout India. While the feast lasted (about one hour), the large feather fans were continually kept wafted just above our heads. On feeling a hand on my shoulder, I turned round at once, and became aware that the black beauty I had risked my life for stood smiling down at me, while wafting the *punka* (fan) over my head. I was afterwards told by Jack Mee that when she supposed no-one was looking, she from time to time pressed her dark lips to the flowers she had placed on my head. The scent which pervaded the entire atmosphere was something almost etherial, and had a sort of dreamy influence about it. I afterwards learnt that it was emitted from the torches which contained a sort of herb.

After the feast was cleared away, the *hookahs* were lighted and passed round, while the circle was enlarged to allow the *noch wallahs* to come in and entertain us. This was done in something like the fashion before described at Rutlam, only on a simpler and less costly scale, but by superior girls, so I thought.

During the whole of this performance

flowers continually rained upon the Englishmen, until we were like water-nymphs, decked with spray jewels. The pretty damsel whom I saved sat at my feet handing me cup after cup of some nice beverage made from fruits, every now and then looking up into my face with such a pleading look shining in her glorious dark and fascinating eyes, until I was almost tempted to forget myself and clasp her in my arms. For I must candidly admit I was hard smitten with this tropical forest beauty, and had she been white instead of dark, there is no saying what the consequences would have been.

I could see she fairly worshipped me, or her lips would not so frequently have been pressed to my hands, riding boots, and other parts of my person, and that she fully intended not to lose sight of me for the remainder of our march will clearly prove, for she gave up forest, home, friends and her sacred caste for the sake of the "white Rajah" and followed us to Ahmednagar where I afterwards procured her a situation as nurse to Mrs. Watson's child, and she still remains with us.

The *ram-sami* finished at about two in

the morning, and we were by no means sorry to reach our camp and bed, and soon were fast asleep, dreaming of the curious affairs of the last few hours.

I forgot to mention that it was the gun of Mr. Oldham which saved me from a cruel death, and he still has the skin of the crocodile's head hanging in his quarters, and whenever I have a look at it I fancy what might have been but for the timely aid of Mr. O.

Tuesday December 2nd.

Our usual morning's packing being finished, we mounted our noble steeds and turned our backs on the beauteous village of the forest where we had been living in a sort of spirit or fairy land, and on turning round after travelling a few hundred yards, I was surprised to see Nana following us. I at once dismounted and went to her and asked her the reason of her following us. Her answer brief and to the point,

"You saved my life, Rajah. I am yours and will ever be with you."

Thus the dark beauty left home, friends

and parents, broke her caste and forsook every endearing thing in her native village for the sake of the white Rajah who had saved her from the cruel jaws of the river monsters. I stopped the baggage wagon and placed her on the top, and we then proceeded on our way.

What a tedious journey we have today; even we, in some parts of the thick forest, have to dismount and fell some trees before our baggage can pass, and in one particular place we had to cross a large bog some three-quarters of a mile across. We all had to set to work felling trees and crossing them with thick branches and bramble with lattice-work of cane, before our baggage could cross.

I can truthfully affirm that I never remember working harder in all my life. After felling trees and placing them so as to form a somewhat solid foundation, I had to go back some few hundred yards and sketch, with reports, the road along which we had come, with full details as to how the battery should proceed.

We scarcely rode above two miles the whole of this day's march, and at 1-30 p.m. we arrived at Sawulda, completely tired out, hungry and thirsty, after a march of nine miles through the most intricate underbush I have ever traversed.

It is almost needless to say that our tent was not pitched. After watering and feeding our horses, we threw down our blankets in the shade of a huge banyan tree, and after a very light breakfast composed of cold meat, bread and not-too-clean water, we dropped ourselves on the blankets and all (Europeans) were quickly asleep, leaving Luximan and Nana to cook our dinner.

About four o'clock in the afternoon we woke up nearly famished, but with the pleasant odour of something good pervading the immediate surroundings, and on learning that some fine goat steaks were frying on the fire, while the smell of good tea met our nasal organs, we at once washed ourselves and made the most of the good things provided for us, and had any decent civilised Christian beheld us at that feast, certainly they would not have thought us fit to grace the table of gentlemen! However, we cared very little about the opinions of the world at that moment; all we considered for the whole of the next half hour was how we could soonest satisfy our internal cravings.

Do not for a moment think, dear readers, that we were trying our best to emulate the wild beasts of these tropical forests; we were merely doing what thousands of other hungry Christians would have done in similar circumstances, merely enjoying a good and well-earned dinner.

I can assure those who have not as yet accomplished a hard day's work in an Indian timber forest that it is not a pleasant matter to toil as we have done that day, and I feel content with our lot in life, with no better reward than the knowledge of having achieved something great for the benefit of those who do not know us, and certainly would not have been much touched had our lives been lost in this enterprise for our Queen and Country; such is the serene countenance of the British Indian Government. However, I will not grumble about my lot; I made my bed, so must do as my Dear Dead Father said—lie upon it. It is no doubt a hard one, but nevertheless 'tis what I myself have manufactured.

Dinner being over, I content myself

with making out my reports until dark, when one and all were by no means displeased to turn in for the night 'neath the kindly shade of the king of forest trees, and having given orders for an early start for tomorrow, we close our eyes in sleep.

Wednesday December 3rd.

It was with great reluctance we left our hard bed this morning, and the daily messenger turned his face to the last camp with anything but pleasure depicted thereon. Well, duty must be done, so we make another start, and it was with feelings of relief that we found our way was somewhat cleaner than the previous day's. We had no felling to do, still, it was not as easy travelling as one could wish, for it was still rather boggy in some places, and many trees had to be marked for the gunners' axe.

I should say we had travelled six or seven miles when the forest ended suddenly, and the clear blue sky could be looked upon again with pleasure. Now on gaining the outskirts of the wood, we became aware of a village, and on

105

approaching we saw six or seven men bearing a corpse towards a large heap of wood close to us. When the wood was ready, the dead body was placed on some large pieces stretched crosswise and saturated with some combustible oil. Then they commenced to build up the remainder of the wood round and over the body. When this was done we were almost frightened out of our wits, and two of our horses broke away, at the wild and weird shrieks of the mourners. When the death-chant subsided, a match was put to the heap, and such a bonfire you never saw, while all round the natives were sallaaming and mourning.

This is another way of burial in this country, something after the fashion of cremation. I have since learnt that the brains and heart and other parts of the burned body are enclosed in gold or silver lockets and presented to the nearest relatives of the deceased.

After some little trouble we caught our refractory steeds and proceeded on our way, and were not sorry to observe that we should not enter the forest again that day.

After about another hour's ride we gained the city of Nuldana after a march of ten miles, well pleased to have accomplished another day's fatigues. So relieving the wants of the horses, we at once pitched our tent and turned our thoughts to the kettle and frypan.

We marched to the farther side of the village or city as they call it, and pitched our camp about a mile away from the wall of the city on account of the horrible stench prevalent in the atmosphere surrounding the city. This, as we afterwards found, was a good thing for us as the following pages will show.

We were in no way molested by the natives, for they scarcely condescended to visit us in small numbers; in fact only one man came near the tent, and he only came to tell us about the forage.

After I had finished making out the reports, I strolled from camp in quest of game. After a walk of about forty minutes I saw a small village about a mile and a half to my right front, and on examining the ground closely, I became aware of a peafowl in the vicinity as every now and then I came across some feathers, so quickly shouldering my gun I turned round and hastened into camp with the good news.

I told the officer, McDonald, and Lawrey the messenger, that we could get the fowl with little trouble, but we should have to be very careful as the natives hereabouts were very strange at the destruction of these birds, so we resolved to strike camp about 8 o'clock that night, then take the baggage a good bit on the way of tomorrow's march, so that we should not be encumbered in our movements if anything serious occurred. We quite expected a scuffle if any of the natives saw us amongst the birds so we made preparations accordingly.

As soon as darkness commenced to set in, we struck camp, and McDonald and myself started with baggage, leaving Mr. O. and Lawrey to reconnoitre the vicinity in which the peafowl lay, arranging to meet at the N.E. corner of the village, and about 300 yards clear of the houses (mud huts), giving them the notes of the cuckoo as my signal.

After travelling about six miles we entered the forest again and finding an uncommon thick and bushy place, I told Mac to keep everything quiet and not to light a fire, and be ready to start at any moment, as I intended to make the next camp before daybreak, so as to have the whole day to rest, for we should need it. After bidding him goodnight, I took my reins well in hand, and started towards our game preserve.

It was fearfully dark; I could scarcely see above ten yards before me in the open, and I wondered how we should manage in the wood; but I satisfied myself that the ground between the village and our baggage in the opposite forest was pretty even so that there would not be much difficulty in trotting if we should wish to.

After about an hour's ride, I was just able to make out the feeble glimmer of the *butti* lights of the village, and another fifteen minutes' cautious travelling brought me within hearing of my colleague's "Cuckoo! Cuckoo!" which I answered in like manner.

"Find a spot, Keates, where we can tether the horses in safety close at hand, so that we shall have no trouble in mounting and getting away at once. I feel

Indian peacock . . . the natives hereabouts were
very strange at the destruction of these birds.

very queer, Keates, somehow; I don't half like the look of the forest where the birds are. It's thick as a hairbrush, and if we get divided it is a case with those who get left behind!"

"Never fear, sir, we shall come out all right. Did you see many birds? How do they lie; pretty well together or straggling?"

"They are pretty well scattered about in the wood, but there are some 20 or 30 nice birds close under the city wall, about 50 yards from it, but it's most infernally dark. Besides, I fancy there is someone knocking about for Lawrey, and I heard someone cough".

"Never mind, we will just empty one barrel each and make for the horses and mount at once; then once off, the whole village can come!" "Hist! What's that? By all the powers of Hades, that is the chink of *tulwa* (sword). Come along quick, and follow me close. Hist! there's some half dozen natives knocking about here. Whereabouts are the thickest lot of birds, sir?" "Here, we are right under 10 or 12 of them, but there's a fellow stands watching us not 12 yards away".

"All right, sir; now do be careful, and whatever you do, don't let them take you, sir. Should you not be able to clear yourself without hurting anyone, make short work of it; and remember if you wound anyone, that dead men tell no tales. And you, Lawrey, keep close to us, and mind where you shoot. Don't forget, Sir, that if there is any dirty work to be done, reserve your fire and take you knife for it, unless too hard-pressed. Here we are, now all fire together and don't leave your game behind. Ready, *fire!*"

Three blinding flashes, five heavy thuds at our feet; but before we could pick up our game we were surrounded by six or seven almost naked natives, and before we could free ourselves they had sent up their infernal blood-curdling whoop which signals all their people who are within hearing.

"To horse, sir, to horse for our lives! Clear yourself; steel, Lawrey, and plenty of it!"

"Oh God—I'm hit, Keates, in the shoulder! They are using their *tulwas!*"

"Use your gun, sir, and club it. I am

pierced in the thigh. Clear away this lot, and we may gain the horses yet in time!"

Bang, Bang, "Let them have it, Lawrey!" *Bang.*

"Now away—club that fellow there, Oldham, or he'll run you through!"

I managed to get two birds, and Lawrey one, and were making as fast as possible towards our horses, when a dark fellow stood across Mr. Oldham's path, his *tulwa* raised ready for striking; so quickly stepping to his rear, I plunged my hunting knife up to the hilt in his left side, and the blade of another native, which had been intended no doubt as my end, fell across my right thumb, cutting through to the bone. After about ten minutes of this horrible work, we succeeded in gaining our horses, and only just in time, for no sooner had we fairly mounted than such a hullaballoo as would have done credit to the inhabitants of Bedlam rent the air, and re-echoed through the dark forest all around.

"Now follow me as closely as possible, and don't be afraid to push your horses, for the ground is pretty even; don't lose that bird, Lawrey, and keep close to Mr. O."

About twenty minutes' sharp gallop brought us to the outskirts of the other forest, where we found McDonald waiting for us, so we at once went to the spot where the baggage had been secreted, and after merely binding up our wounds without our native followers knowing anything about it, or our doings, we at once started for our next camp. After a tedious march of five miles through intricate forest trees and creepers we came out on to a very small plain, on the further side of which stood the city of Sonegar; and thinking it advisable to lie quiet through the day, we pitched our camp in the shelter of the forest.

As soon as our tent was pitched, and cattle cared for, we went to a small stream some few yards from camp, taking our medicine chest with us. On properly examining our wounds, it was seen that Mr. Oldham had a very severe slash across the back of his left shoulder, and a slight cut with the point of a *tulwa* in the left arm. His shirt, flannel and jacket were soaked with blood, and it is certain from his weak state that he had lost a fair amount, as also was the case with myself, having a severe wound in the right thigh, and another, not very dangerous one, in the fleshy part of my right thumb. However, a good bath in the stream did us good, after which I stitched up the slash in the officer's shoulder, dressed both his and my own wounds, and returned to the tent where we found a good breakfast awaiting us.

We had arrived in this camp about four o'clock, just before break of day, so that we should have a good day's rest before us, and we needed it. Lawrey escaped with a slight scalp wound, which, had it not been for his forage cap, might have been more serious.

We kept very quiet all that day, McDonald only leaving the camp for forage, and Lawrey, as soon as the sun rose, went back with reports, but we gave him a circuitous route by which to go and return, with a surmised route some two miles west of Nuldana, for the Battery, having well studied the map to see that no serious obstacle should impede their way.

The whole of our day, after making our reports and pegging out the ground for the main body, was spent in smoking, sleeping, and drinking tea. Our appetites had completely forsaken us, and our wounds were smarting frightfully. We quite expected to have some trouble with them through giving them no rest, but this could not be helped as we must not go sick now, or we should certainly condemn ourselves. Besides, we wished to take the battery safe to Ahmednagar, so we resolved that unless absolutely compelled, we would not give in.

We had decided to deny any knowledge whatever of the little skirmish which had nearly cost us so dear, and being aware that our followers were ignorant of our doings, this was quite easy.

Friday December 5th.

Found Mr. O. and I very sore indeed, and very loath to leave our couch, but when Jack Mee arrived in camp just before we finished our cup of tea, with the news that the natives of Sonegar district were scouring the country in search of some *Bliti* (Englishmen), we thought it best to clear out as speedily as possible.

Packing our baggage and saddling our horses, we left Sonegar as quickly and quietly as possible, and after a very painful and tedious march of fourteen miles, we came in sight of the city of Dhulia.

After breakfast I limped, for I could not walk, into the city, and found it a very large, busy and seemingly clean place, with about 20,000 inhabitants. Their chief occupation is cotton spinning, for Dhulia is the centre of the Indian cotton cultivation, and thousands upon thousands of bales of this stuff come into the city weekly. There are also linen manufacturers here, one or two of which we were invited to overlook. The work is done much in the same manner as in English factories, the only difference being the colour of the employees.

We were each presented with half a dozen handkerchiefs, which proved on inspection to be much inferior to European goods, however we accepted them and returned to camp rather tired after the stroll, and as dinner was ready when we reached the tent, we did justice to the good things Luximan had prepared for us.

We did not leave camp again that day.

After making out our reports the time was spent pretty much as usual, while the silent intervals were filled up now and again with a muttered curse from Mr. O. or myself at our ill luck, and when darkness closed in we were by no means sorry to avail ourselves of the little luxury our none too easy couch afforded us.

Saturday December 6th.

Morning broke bright and calm, and we left our beds somewhat refreshed after a good night's sleep, in spite of the pain the wounds of our *Satara* escapade procured for us.

We marched very quickly today, for none of us seemed in any humour for conversation; indeed scarcely anything but monosyllables were uttered until we came to the banks of the river Taptee. This was slow work crossing, as the river sides were so dreadfully uneven, and we were not sorry when our poor horses got beyond their depth, for their legs trembled awfully. However, we did cross over safe, and without leaving the saddle, and when the baggage was safely over we pitched our camp some four hundred yards from the bank of the river, and about half a mile from Arvi, a distance of 19 miles from Dhulia.

Much of this morning is spent in tending our wounds, and both Mr. Oldham and myself were not surprised to see our cuts somewhat inflamed. However, we hoped to get down the inflammation during today and tomorrow.

MacDonald, and Lawrey, who caught us up at the river bank, were kind enough to do the washing for the whole family today, while Jack Mee went out in quest of something to satisfy the inner man. And on his return at sunset we settled down to spend a pleasant evening in the hopes that we might forget our pain in the merriment. Never was I more tempted to enjoy a drop of whisky than I was tonight, but I managed to overcome the longing. I fancy it was the peg of port and brandy that Mr. O. and I took at the completion of every day's march, to strengthen us and make up for the severe loss of blood both had sustained.

I almost forgot to mention that Lawrey brought a full detailed report of the Satara affray back from the battery, and that the District agent would interview us on Sunday. It appears that two natives were killed and three wounded, one very severely; but from Mee's account, which he brought the previous day from the billeting party, we shall not be suspected of the affair, as the wounded natives swear to twelve or even more Europeans attacking them! So if nothing is known by our followers, which I think is the case, then we are all right.

After seeing that everything which might condemn us is out of sight, we settled down for a pleasant smoke and chat while supper was served, when all did their best to enjoy it; after which blankets were spread, pipes lighted, and ears ready for. . . .

Lawrey's tale

"WELL, boys, you all know, before I came in the army I belonged to the merchant service, and while abroad I saw some queer things. You all know that sailors are very superstitious chaps, and are often very stubborn when their fancy happens to play them false.

Now while our ship was frozen in one winter for four months off Antwerp, I was one night doing first watch. The rest of the crew except the cook had gone ashore. I had been pacing the deck for some time, smoking and musing upon one strange thing or another, when I was startled by hearing a voice by my side mutter the command, "Follow me!" and jumping round in my excitement I thought I saw a white figure drop over the bows into the water, and I distinctly heard a splash in the water beneath. All was inky darkness all around, except the glimmer of the shore lights surrounding us. I hastened to the ship's side, and there in the water not twelve boats' length from our barque, was a white struggling figure. I hastily took off my jacket, dived in to the rescue, leaving the ship in the hands of the cook.

When I reached the surface again I made out the figure, slowly struggling in and out of the great ice-floes, gradually towards the shore. I was a pretty strong swimmer, but I did not seem to gain on the subject of my sympathy. At last I saw it step out on to a large sheet of ice, turn round and beckon me, and, shivering all over, I at last gained the same piece of ice, but found to my dismay that the figure had reached the quayside and was still beckoning me. Come what may, I could not shake off the fascination of her eyes which gleamed like living coals. Onward glided the spirit form, in whose train I followed with chattering teeth, dripping clothes, and a fearful presentiment of evil, but I could not shake off the magnetic power of those eyes.

How many streets, by-ways and lanes we traversed I know not, but at last we came out on to a country road shaded by tall overhanging trees. We must have trudged along this lane for a full mile and a half when the figure, which had kept always some yards ahead of me, stopped, beckoned me again, then pointed to something on the ground, then disappeared as suddenly as it had appeared.

I hastened up to the spot on which she had stood, and there, lying in the roadside, was a human figure in deathly stillness. I stooped down and put my hand to the heart,

"Ah! He lives!"

I lifted his head up, rubbed his hands, and looked for somewhere to procure assistance, but nothing, except a glimmering light about 3 or 4 hundred yards away, met my anxious eyes. However, I thought, where that light is must surely be some living creature, so I was just about to leave my charge to enquire into it when a groan escaped the prostrate figure before me. I called to him to speak, and in a half-conscious muttering he asked for water. Water I had not, so I gave him what answered his purpose just as well, a bit of ice.

Slowly he opened his eyes, slightly raised his head, and in very good English asked where he was. Now here was a poser: how did I know? All I could say was, "in Europe". After a bit he got upon his feet and staggered forward, but I took his arm in time, or he would have fallen.

He continually kept putting his hand to his head, and then I noticed for the first time a dark stain down the side of his face. I put my fingers on it and traced the dark stream to a frightful gash in his head.

"A bit of foul play here, mate? Who's been spoiling your figurehead?"

"Never mind, I'll be even with them yet, curse them! They thought to finish me, but I'm made of tougher stuff than that."

"Let us get off to a place where your wound can be dressed a bit!"

"No! put this handkerchief round it, and if you are the man I take you to be, you'll help me to pursue these scoundrels who have done this, and also rob them of the pleasure they anticipated from Lidia Halford, whom they took away to some place in the city, but I fancy I know where they are. There's an old gambling hell in a

124

low quarter, bearing a very dark character, where I once remember seeing the two cowards who made this mess of me. If you will help me tonight, my man, I will make it worth your while. As you surmise, I am an Englishman bred and born, and of good family, but for one purpose or another I spend most of my time over here, and not in the best of ways either. The girl I had with me tonight though has nothing whatever to do with my life. She is a countrywoman of ours, is a governess to an English family staying here, and while taking a stroll this evening I saw her struggling with these two men whom we are now going to seek. As a rule I never interfere in any rows of this sort, but when it comes to seeing one of my own countrywomen in the hands of such thoroughgoing rogues as I knew the men to be, of course I stepped in to the rescue, and this is what I got. However, it's ony lent, and I'll pay it back too, with interest!"

Thus as we talked, we had reached a very quiet part of the city, and my companion at last thought he had found the right quarter, so procuring the services of two gendarmes we turned down a very dark street, or I might say alley, of which this quarter of Antwerp is chiefly composed. After my companion had been eagerly scanning the dens on either side of the street, he paused suddenly and exclaimed,

"That's the place! Now you two officers, take the back and front door between you, while we enter the house and look around; and if I shout for help, come at once, and not unless."

My companion gave some peculiar signal at the door with a stick which we had procured on the road, and in a few minutes the door was opened by a rather elderly female. After a few words between them which I could not understand, we were shown upstairs, but no light seemed to be visible about the place. When we reached the landing at the top of two flights of stairs, we came to a door on our right, and my friend knocked.

"Now, my friend", said the man, "we shall no doubt have a struggle, but we shall manage them, I think, for there are only the two of them and the girl".

Our knock was answered by a gruff, "Who's that?" to which my companion answered in some more of the language I had heard him speak to the woman.

At last someone opened the door, but slightly, and no sooner was this done than both of us rushed at the door together, knocking down the man who opened it, and we entered the room.

What a sight met our eyes! Sitting in one corner of the room was a beautiful woman, partially naked, with her hands and legs tied to the chair, and her mouth gagged. On the table were bottles and glasses of spirits, cards, dice and stilettos. On one side of the table stood a dark foreigner who had risen and grasped his weapon at our entrance, and the man who had opened the door stood on the opposite side of the table and would have taken up his weapon had not my stout cudgel descended on his rather delicate hand, breaking two of his fingers. My companion had locked the door and taken the key, after which he turned to his cowardly would-be murderers saying,

"You thought to end me, did you? It's my turn now, and I'm going to pay off old scores. So, you dastardly imps, you were interested in a pleasant game, eh? And the stakes? A pure woman's virtue. Ah well, you are beaten this time!

"Put down that knife, my boy, or I shall have no mercy, for if you attempt any violence I will spread your cowardly brains on the floor. Thanks, now we'll show you how a British soldier and sailor can avenge an insult!"

As my friend said this he dealt the darker of the two men a fearful blow in the face which sent him reeling across the room. I could not resist following his good example, so laid the other fellow low. When we had bound them, we liberated the girl, then calling in the officers, we handed them over to justice. A few days after they were tried and sentenced to twelve months' imprisonment; not half enough, by the Lord Harry, they should have had that number of years.

It is needless to say I was never without a glass of grog while the ice lasted, and my companion, who I learnt had been an officer in the English army but had to leave it for some scandal, soon after married the governess when they returned to England. I often went to see them whenever I went to Woolwich, but I have never seen them since I joined the Army myself; but if I live to get home again I will go again and see the man I saved from death and the woman I saved from dishonour.

"Good Night, chaps!"

"Good Night, Lawrey."

"Good Night!"

We asked him in the morning if he ever saw the woman in white again, but he seemed offended at the question, so we did not bother him about the ghost again!

Sunday December 7th.

Was spent very much in the usual manner. Captain Williamson, the District Government agent, spent the best part of the day with us, but whether he was under any impression of our guilt we could not say; I think not, for he chatted, smoked, and thoroughly enjoyed himself till evening, when he shook hands with all and bade us a safe march to 'Nagar. He informed us that he did not often have the pleasure of leading a thorough jungle life, but he had enjoyed himself immensely during the day, and indeed, when evening came, he seemed very loth to leave us.

Monday December 8th.

Morning broke, as usual, bright and calm, and after the usual routines of packing etc., we turned our backs on Arvi and settled down to a steady trot through a totally different sort of country from which we had been struggling for the last week or two. We were still amongst hills, but the surrounding scenery and cultivation was something marvellous, in fact if you look at the rough side of a cow hide you will see every bit as much as we saw this day, ground never was so void of vegetation.

The sun was up very early this morning and almost on his first appearance we felt his warmth, and when he had fairly risen in the heavens it became very warm; in fact it was uncomfortably so. However, after marching through this desert sort of country for about 12½ miles we rode into Jhoregon, tired and hungry, and I was suffering great pain from my wounds as also was Mr. O. on account of the intense heat, and the glitter of the scorching sand reflected the brilliancy of the sun so strongly that even through our shaded glasses our eyes were sorely tried.

I assure you that we were not very long in pitching our tent and making the most of its kindly shelter, while our breakfast was speedily prepared by our worthy butler.

It is not necessary to state that except for making out our reports we did nothing at all today but get what little pleasure we were able to draw out of our pipes and the tea pot; and when the sun had hidden his burning face behind the distant hills we gave our horses a feed of corn and a drink, and after partaking of some light refreshment ourselves we lay down to enjoy a good night's rest.

Tuesday December 9th.

Finds us again in the saddle, and the cool morning air is truly refreshing, quite a contrast to yesterday. Reason?—simply because we had some rain during the night, and the horses and men quite enjoy the good effects of the change.

I forgot to mention that for the past few days the water has been very bad, and hay or grass for horses cannot possibly be procured, so that we are compelled to resort to extra grain for the beasts, and much to our regret we learn that there is still a greater scarcity of both water and forage further on.

There is nothing of interest to note today, except that, after about 5 miles' march, McDonald shot a splendid *Eilghi* (wild bull) which was a good addition to our larder, for we had been confined pretty much to goat's flesh these few days past, with a few birds for supper now and then.

We reached Malegaon after 18 miles ride through a very uninteresting country. Malegaon was not a very likely place from the exterior of the city, but on entering, which we did after breakfast, we were quite surprised to find that we had dropped into a rather enlightened place. What I mean by enlightened is in respect to architecture which was of a very substantial kind, not the mud-and-plaster, soon-tumble, pig-and-hen sort of abodes. There were many of the latter to be seen about, outside the radius of the city proper, but the city itself contained good, strong and well-built edifices, with a good breadth in the majority of the streets, and after I had taken a few sketches, we returned to camp.

Wednesday December 10th.

Well, to tell the truth, dear readers, I don't really know how properly to describe the disasters of the night, but after due consideration I have decided to relate, in simple form, what happened after we retired to rest last night. In the first place we were awakened by a fearful clap of thunder, and almost before we could properly open our eyes, a terrific hurricane, or what is called in this country a typhoon, swept across us. It tore our tent away from its pegs and left us standing in the heaviest shower of rain I ever beheld, and I have seen a few big ones too. Action was useless, we could do nothing. The soaking ground let go the pegs to which our horses were picketed, and the poor animals, what with the fearfully vivid lightning, heavy peals of thunder, and deluge of falling water, were almost mad with fear, and to tell you the real truth, the lot of us were somewhat scared. There were we, in total darkness, in a strange place, the water, which could not get away fast enough, gradually rising till it reached our knees, wet through, our tent blown away, and every now and then the lightning would reveal our horses wildly galloping across the plain—thus I leave you to guess how miserable we were. Never yet was man in worse and more helpless circumstances, and how on earth we managed to get all together again this morning, Goodness only knows, but we did manage it, and at about 12 o'clock today we were ready for a start, and after about 14 miles' tiring march under the scorching rays of a tropical sun, we arrived at Julgaum, about 3 o'clock p.m.

There is nothing of interest to speak of in this place, except a fine bridge which crosses the river. What few things we had not dried in the morning were laid out in the sun, while we got a bit of refreshment and rest which we wanted very badly.

The messenger who visited the main body reported that only two tents were left standing; the whole of the horses were loose, and every man Jack wet through to the skin. The major's tent also blew down while he and Mrs. Watson were asleep and nearly smothered them. They were also wet through and lost a lot of their camp furniture.

Thursday December 11th.

We make one more start for another day's fatigues, and after about an hour's ride, find ourselves among the hills again. It was rather a picturesque march today, but somehow or other none of us seemed at all interested in it. To tell the truth we were pretty well sick and tired of the tedious day-after-day fatigues and unrest, and we were one and all anxiously awaiting the end of it.

At the end of each day for the last week, life had been more or less a misery to Mr. O. and myself. Our wounds were getting worse each day owing to the constant exertions.

We halted for lunch about half way as usual, and after 30 minutes' rest we proceeded on our way, and entered Munmar, having accomplished 13 miles, so deciding to rest for the day here, the tent was pitched and our usual duties done.

Munmar is a great stopping station for the GIP Railway, and it was quite a relief to see some fresh white faces again, after being, as it were, shut out from the world for so long. I took several sketches here. The Temperance Choir of the battery gave us an entertainment here and were well received.

Friday December 12th.

The old familiar shriek of the engine whistle brought to our minds the fact that morning had arrived, and with it our usual starting time, so going through the now monotonous duties before-mentioned, we bestride our patient animals and again seek for pastures green, and adventures new (but didn't want the latter).

I might save both myself further trouble and you uninterestedness, by saying at once that this march was like the majority of others before described "void of interest", so after saying that we arrived safe at Sawurgaum, I'll close for the day.

Saturday December 13th.

This day proved very interesting to us all, and more especially to Mr. O. and myself, for we saw a sight that will never leave my memory. I have often heard of a mirage, but never witnessed one till now. After leaving Sawurgaum, in which place we could scarcely get any water, while that we had for both man and horse was got from small pits dug in the earth, and it was just like drinking mud, or rather eating mud —we had gone about 9 miles when we came out on a beautiful plain, level as a billiard table, but void of vegetation or anything green whatever, and the heat from the burning sand rendered the air suffocating, while the reflection of the sun almost blinded us. Well, I say we had travelled about 9 miles without seeing a drop of water of any description, while horses and men were parched and almost choking for want of water, while not a sign of anything like liquid was visible, when Mr. O. shook my arm, and pointing his finger to our right front, exclaimed, "Water!"

I took my glasses and eagerly scanned the surrounding country, and there, to our right front, about three miles away, was to be seen what appeared to us a large crystal-like sheet of water, so urging on our poor steeds, we made for the anticipated pleasure of a beautiful drink. Alas for the delusions of humanity, after travelling for about an hour in the direction of what we thought was water, we were utterly tired out, parched tongues and mouths panting for a drink, with the disheartening fact staring us in the face that no water was to be seen. However, at that moment we saw a string of camels coming towards us, some two miles further on, so mounting our poor steeds again, we go to meet the desert steeds whose drivers give us information that some six miles further on was a small *Toptee Tope* (grove) where we should find some water tanks, but with very little water, and that was bad. They also told us that for many miles along the road they had come there was a great scarcity of *pawnee* (water).

With what sad hearts we turned our faces for the *toptee tope* can be better imagined than described. I will say, though, that under such trying circumstances both men and cattle behaved in grand style.

Perhaps men who understand horses will, reading this book, think our beasts but poor ones, to be knocked up after about 18 miles' march, but when you understand the difficulty to be contended with on the march in East India, you will make some allowance for the straits in which we found ourselves that day. I can say with truth that we have been travelling with our horses over their fetlocks in scorching sand, over six or seven miles, and more than once too, finishing up with about five or six miles of hard flint rock, where the poor animals could scarcely stand on their poor scorched feet.

Many of you may imagine you would like to be on such an expedition as this; doubtless you would, and the next time I am detailed for this duty I will give you an invitation, and should you wish, you may take my place: then tell me what you think of the pleasures of an Indian Reconnaissance March!

There are many more little disagreeable things I might mention here, but I do not wish to dishearten would-be enterprising heroes.

Suffice it to say, then, that we reached the *toptee tope*, and found as was told us, only sufficient water to last the battery horses two days by allowing each beast one gallon per day, while men had to do with less than a pint per day for the purpose of drinking and washing, and what there was of it was not fit even to wash in, and that is the truth; however, we had to make the most of it.

After securing our horses and pitching our tent, we had a reconnoitre around the vicinity, and found that water was not to be seen anywhere, neither was forage in the shape of grass. All we could get was grain; that was obtained from a city some eight miles to our left, and then there was not sufficient to give full measures to the battery cattle.

After an early tea, we saddled our horses and went out as far as Nodis to order what corn could be got for the horses, and did not return till late at night, so after a good supper (which we much enjoyed) and a smoke with a couple of songs, we turned in without our usual yarn, so you must fancy one for yourselves this week, my friends; and with good wishes for a peaceful sleep to all we bid you and the world Good Night.

Sunday December 14th

We rise at our usual Sabbath hour, and after enjoying our breakfast off boiled grouse and pigeon, washed down by a drop of coffee, we sally out with dogs and guns to see what luck shall reward our searchings, for our larder is miserably bare today.

We get into a rather deep *nullah* (ravine) some three miles through the *tope*, and after dropping a few birds, hare, and gathering a few herbs, we were about to return for camp when we noticed the prints of a cheetah's pad in the sand, which seemed to be new. We none of us felt very eager for large game, but as we had dropped accidentally across his track we decided to follow it up for a bit and see what it was.

About 1½ miles from where his print was first noticed, we came to a bit of very thick jungle, with many deep fissures much overgrown by underbush, and all about the place was strewn with the bones of many animals, and above one head of a human being met our searching eyes. After traversing this semi-darkness arcade for some few hundred years, we came between two high walls of rock forming a sort of passage; so before going any further, we thought it advisable to load our pieces with ball. We had scarcely completed this operation, when from very close to where we stood proceeded a terrific growl which startled us to almost drop our pieces, and we were only just prepared in time to meet the enemy, when from out of a small cave to our right issued as fine a cheetah as ever man clapped his eyes on, and he seemed as unconcerned at our presence as if we were mice instead of men. However, we did not give him much time for meditation, for Mr. O. and I, who were both loaded with express slug, gave him the deadly contents of our barrels. He made one terrific bound and dropped dead at our feet.

To turn him over and skin him was our next move, and after about half an hour's tough work, his skin was off, rolled and ready for the return journey to camp. This was the only animal of this description we have been able to kill, though we had been in their vicinity two or three times, but we had not the time to devote to the chase as we might have wished. We shot several black wolves and also hyenas, so we were rather proud of the success we had achieved today, and our spirits were high.

We arrived in camp, gave over the spoils of war to the cook, and after dressing our wounds again, which by the bye had not been improved by our ramble, we set about curing the skin of our great capture.

We spent the remainder of the day in our usual fashion, and when night had fairly set in we had supper, packed our baggage, and retired to rest, all feeling quite capable of enjoying the undisturbed slumber we anticipated, and which our day's work had very well earned. At all events we bade each other good night, and turned in to try our luck.

Monday December 15th.

We were up and away in good time today as we expected a long and tedious march to go through; and after turning our backs on Kopergaum we urge our fresh steeds on to a smart trot, all feeling in pretty good spirits, considering the distressing circumstances under which we have been travelling for the past few days. It is quite unnecessary to inform my readers that, though our spirits were somewhat higher than usual, it was not because our wounds were any the less painful—those of Mr. Oldham and myself I mean; and those who had none to aggravate them were almost as miserable with anxiety and sympathy for us.

The reason of our present light-heartedness is that our troubles are speedily to an end, for in the course of three or four more days we anticipate an entrance into our long looked-for-goal—Ahmednagar. And you, my dear readers, I am sure, will heartily echo our most earnest prayers—that we may arrive safe at our destination, with success attending our every effort to do our duty as Englishmen and British Soldiers.

Thus we journeyed on, enjoying a smoke, laugh and joke as we proceed, trying to buoy up our hearts as much as possible.

Having travelled a distance of 22 miles we came to a small village, and finding little water, which was very bad, we thought it advisable to remain at Rahata (Burra) for today, as it was quite possible we might go further and fare worse.

Tuesday December 16th.

Finds us again on the move, and after marching about 6 miles we cross the river Godovari. This is a rather slow-running river, about 1¼ mile across and 13 feet in the deepest part. After seeing our baggage safely over, we proceed, until arriving at Kolhar, having completed 19 miles that day, over some very barren country.

Kolhar is not a very large place but a rather picturesque one, so I have decided to give you an idea of Indian landscape again. There is nothing to interest you here so I shall close this day's march.

Wednesday December 17th.

Having started on our way, the morning's messenger informs us that he has had bad news from the main body, and all were eager to learn it. It appears that some of the men with the battery had been eating some very ripe fruit at Kopergaum, after which they drank a lot of water in the sun, the water being very bad as will be seen in our report of that day. Several of them became very ill, and two of them died during the night and were buried early next morning.

This news, as you would expect, damped our spirits somewhat for a time; however, coming into Nimbadaira, after a march of 16 miles, we were a little merrier, almost forgetting the late sad death of two more of our comrades.

Nimbadaira is a very pretty place. We spent the greater part of today looking through our glasses at our long looked-for destination, which we could plainly see in the distance, and we were all as light-hearted as could be expected.

In the cool of the evening we set about making ourselves and our equipment look a bit respectable so that we might not be taken for the "Forlorn Hope" when marching into Ahmednagar; and after having a good look round our camp to see that all was correct, we went in to supper, over which, and our pipes, we talked over our tomorrow's expected pleasures and reception. All seemed in good spirits, even Mr. Oldham and myself enjoyed a good hearty laugh or two at the jokes which every now and then dropped from members of our party.

Thursday December 18th.

Saw us astir very early, for we intended trotting into A'Nagar pretty sharp. So at 3-30 prompt we left our camp ground at Nimbadaira, by the light of the waning moon, and after a run of 17 miles we entered the city of Ahmednagar, having been on the road 2 hours and 30 minutes.

Early as we had arrived, we were received by the Governors etc. of the place, who had received notice of our approach from the outpost mounted police.

When we had arrived within three miles of A'Nagar, we were challenged by the mounted hill police, in the "Borce pass" and on learning that we were the advance party of the Battery, one mounted man hastened off at full gallop to notify the authorities of our coming.

Having dismounted, looked at ourselves and equippage, we rode into 'Nagar, and were met by nearly the whole European populace of the Station. After taking our horses to stables which had been kindly lent by different officers of the Station, we were one and all invited to the Mess of the Royal Lancashire Fusiliers, where we enjoyed a stunning breakfast.

At 8 o'clock we were warned for the Brigade Officer, to give in our reports etc. after which we were invited to spend the remainder of the day at a garden party given in honour of our safe arrival in the station; and I can assure you, we all thoroughly enjoyed ourselves.

Mr. O. and myself had been to the hospital in the morning and had our wounds properly attended to, and not before they wanted it, for we were both in a critical state. Mr. O. in fact was unable to proceed to Poona for the ensuing Camp of Exercise, and only by very hard entreaties from my Commanding Officer— Major Watson—was I permitted to finish the full Reconnaissance of the March; and on our arrival at Poona early in January, I was compelled to give in and go to Hospital, and once or twice it was feared I should lose my leg; and all through my own neglect.

Mr. Oldham has not even now throughly recovered from his wounds, and anticipates going on leave to recruit his health and strength.

The main body remained in 'Nagar until the 26th. December. They enjoyed a pretty fair Christmas in spite of difficulties. I rode into camp and spent the greater part of Christmas Day there, Major and the Hon. Mrs. Watson kindly inviting me to remain for dinner with them. I did so, and after singing a few Temperance songs with our Battery Temperance Choir, I saddled my horse and rode back to my own party at Sichala, a distance of 18 miles, arriving there about 12 midnight, completely tired out. Poor old Jack Mee was looking out for me, and met me with a lantern about half a mile from camp, whither he led my exhausted steed and its tired rider.

Thus ends my description of a battery's march in India. And trusting that all mistakes and faults in the writing and illustrations will be leniently dealt with, and that your criticisms will not be allowed to have full play in judging the works of a young author,

I beg to remain,
Dear Readers,
Yours Most Respectfully,

Driver C. Keates,
Reconnaissance Clerk,
26th. Field Battery, RA
Ahmednagar, November 21st. 1891

Epilogue

. . . I've traversed jungle paths,
Sweetheart, I've sought the tiger's lair.

What I see abroad, Sweetheart

You ask me where I've been,
   sweetheart?
I've wandered o'er the sea,
I travelled o'er dark India's plain,
And long to be with thee.
You ask me what I've seen,
   sweetheart,
Across the mighty deep;
I saw the sun-scorched arid plains,
Where many comrades sleep.

I've traversed jungle paths,
   sweetheart,
I've sought the tiger's lair.
I saw his lifeless carcase stretched
Beside the mountain bear.
I wandered by Nerbudda's banks,
And watched its cruel force
Snatch fiercely as it sped along

A comrade from his horse.*

I saw the trembling tears, sweetheart,
Roll down a brother's cheek,
Who saw his only brother drowned,
Oh, pray call him not weak.
I saw some curious cities, love,
Where dark-skinned creatures dwell,
Who for the smallest bit of gold
Their own black babes would sell.

I saw the jungle fowl, sweetheart,
I have plucked the eagle's plume;
I've slept beneath the waving palm,
Night, morning, and at noon.
I stood beside the moonlit lake,
And watched the wild goose sport.
I've set the snares with skilful hand,
By which these birds are caught.

I've tracked the noble buck,
    sweetheart,
Across the scorching plain;

* The late Driver Frank Viggars, who was accidentally drowned while crossing the Nerbudda with his
horses. (Page 69).

I lifted up my face to heaven,
And called in vain for rain.
I cannot tell you all I've seen
In this strange sunny land;
But what I have not seen, but missed,
Are thy sweet face and hand.

From: *Memoirs of Strange Lands*
by *C. Keates*

Chums

What cheer, my old companion,
My comrade staunch and true,
From many a plain and hilltop
We've had a bird's eye view,
Since first we drove together
The Royal Artillery guns,
And together learnt our foot-drill
Which found us first good chums.

Two years' eventful journey
Our memory still revives,
How well we've stuck together,
And will do all our lives.
We have in days of sickness,
When health us rudely shuns,
Stuck staunchly to each other,
Like true and faithful chums.

Ah Jack! what many changes
Have passed since we were lads,
We've left our friends far off, boy,
And both have lost our dads.

But, Jack, we'll stick together,
No matter what change comes,
And share alike misfortunes,
As good old English chums.

What would our many friends say,
Could they but see us now?
So far away from loved ones,
As we wipe our heated brow.
Could they but see our faces
Down which the salt tear runs,
They would think and say together,
"There's two good honest chums".

Then, with our hands extended,
The heart with friendship burns,
Which through our wandering ever
Has met with staunch returns.

And Jack, may our alliance
Exist till death o'ercomes
The weary feeble footsteps
Of we two faithful chums.

Dedicated to my dear friend
and comrade, John Mee.
C. Keates,
26th. Field Battery RA
Neemuch, East India
29th October 1889

A Soldier's Prayer

In the broad jungle dark,
There is no light,
Where a lone soldier sat
Throughout the night.
His eyes red with weeping,
He fain would be sleeping
As bent was his head;
King death had bereft him,
His brightness had left him,
His father was dead.

Then a bright vision came,
Would it were true,
Scenes that were far away
Clearly to view.
Rocks seemed to be riven,
Revealing bright Heaven,
He starts at the sight.
There in the starry sky
Watched he with loving eye
His loved ones by night.

Then o'er the desert dark
Cometh a light;
Deep in his soul it sinks,
Beautiful, bright.
Then his heart with joy swelling,
He longed to be dwelling
With his father up there.
With heart full to rending,
His knees humbly bending,
He breathes forth a prayer.

"Father of Heaven! Ruler of the
    storm!
Look down with pity on this prostrate
    form;
Turn not away thine eye from my
    distress,
Look down with pity, to pardon and
    bless.
I ask not for lighter burden to bear,
But, Oh Loved Redeemer, list to my
    prayer.
Hark to my pleading for those o'er the
    foam,
Who are anxiously waiting to welcome
    me home.

Guard my dear mother and keep her
from harm,
And to sisters and brothers let life e'er
be calm.
Give my heart courage, should I have
to fight,
Let my trust be in Thee, and for the
right.
But if I fall in War, if such thy will
be,
Then, Oh, My Gracious God, bring
me to thee.
Look now with mercy, from Heavenly
vault,
Let my repentant tears wash out every
fault.
Teach me to live, my inmost heart to
train,
So that when we are called, we may
all meet again."

Then as the morning broke,
Joyous and bright,
There the lone soldier sat,
Cheered by the light.
The tall palms were rustling,
All nature seemed bustling,
As he lists to a bird,

Whose notes sweetly ringing,
Seemed now to be singing,
"Thy prayer shall be heard".

Clifford Keates

Composed after going into the jungle to hide his grief on hearing the news of his father's death. (Thomas Keates died on August 21st. 1889).

Clifford Keates' prize-winning entry in a Poona art exhibition 1893.

ROYAL ARTILLERY THEATRE.

AHMEDNAGAR.

By kind permission of

Major H. Brackenbury Royal Artillery.

Commanding 26th Field Battery. R. A.

The Amateur Minstrel & Variety Troupe will give an Entertainm

BY SPECIAL REQUEST.

ON

Monday 14th August 1893.

PRICES OF ADMISSION.

Front Seats Rs. 1.
Second   ,,   As. 8.
Third   ,,   As. 4.

TICKETS From Pay Sergts. of Corps.

DOORS open at 8-45 P. M.

Commencing at 9-15 P. M.

Front cover of a programme in which Clifford Keates featured as an entertainer.

162

GUIDE
TO THE COLOUR CODING
OF
ULVERSCROFT BOOKS

Many of our readers have written to us expressing their appreciation for the way in which our colour coding has assisted them in selecting the Ulverscroft books of their choice. To remind everyone of our colour coding— this is as follows:

BLACK COVERS
Mysteries

★

BLUE COVERS
Romances

★

RED COVERS
Adventure Suspense and General Fiction

★

ORANGE COVERS
Westerns

★

GREEN COVERS
Non-Fiction

NON-FICTION TITLES
in the
Ulverscroft Large Print Series

FICTION TITLES
in the
Ulverscroft Large Print Series

MYSTERY TITLES
in the
Ulverscroft Large Print Series